Order this book online at www.trafford.com/06-3000
or email orders@trafford.com

Most Trafford titles are also available at major online book retailers.

Note for Librarians: A cataloguing record for this book is available from Library
and Archives Canada at www.collectionscanada.ca/amicus/index-e.html

Printed in Victoria, BC, Canada.

ISBN: 978-1-4251-1241-7

*We at Trafford believe that it is the responsibility of us all, as both individuals
and corporations, to make choices that are environmentally and socially sound.
You, in turn, are supporting this responsible conduct each time you purchase a
Trafford book, or make use of our publishing services. To find out how you are
helping, please visit www.trafford.com/responsiblepublishing.html*

*Our mission is to efficiently provide the world's finest, most comprehensive
book publishing service, enabling every author to experience success.
To find out how to publish your book, your way, and have it available
worldwide, visit us online at www.trafford.com/10510*

 www.trafford.com

North America & international
toll-free: 1 888 232 4444 (USA & Canada)
phone: 250 383 6864 ♦ fax: 250 383 6804 ♦ email: info@trafford.com

The United Kingdom & Europe
phone: +44 (0)1865 722 113 ♦ local rate: 0845 230 9601
facsimile: +44 (0)1865 722 868 ♦ email: info.uk@trafford.com

10 9 8 7 6 5

Contents

About the Author

The author has always been a huge fan of Hollywood and of the Entertainment Industry in general but not of its trappings She has a legal background and is of South American and African Ancestry. She grew up with a very loving Mother and an award winning Journalist Father. She is married with children. She spends a lot of time in the United Kingdom where she also received an education at Cambridge University.

Dedication

This book is dedicated to my mother for giving me life and showing me what true love really means and to my children for choosing me to be their own mummy and especially the little one for keeping me awake so many nights this year that I was compelled to write this book.

1

Their Life Stories, A Synopsis

Jennifer "Jen" Aniston:

Jennifer Aniston was born on February 11 1969 in Sherman Oaks California. Her Mom (Nancy) was an actress/model, her Dad (John Aniston) was an actor of Greek descent who worked mainly on television. John Aniston was born Yiannis Anastassakis in the small town of Crete in Greece.

He moved to the United States with his Parents when he was ten years old. He later joined the United States Navy and worked as an Intelligence Officer in Panama where he attained the position of Lieutenant Commander prior to becoming an actor. Her Godfather was Telly Savalas. She had that in common with a desperate housewife, Nicolette Sheridan. Her father left her mother for another woman after twelve years of Marriage. No child can be happy about this and she wasn't. She later said that to take her mind off things, She used to pretend to be Bionic woman as a child. During her childhood, the family relocated to Greece where she lived for a year before returning to the United States.

She developed an interest in acting at an early age and in 1984 attended the La Guardia High School of Performing Arts in New York graduating in 1987. She moved back to Hollywood when she was twenty. She was a part time waitress and appeared in a couple of failed television shows before 'Friends' came calling.

From all accounts, Jennifer was not the typical Hollywood type that enjoyed the serial or casual dating scene. Her boyfriends seemed to come few and far between. She showed a preference for rock stars at some point in her life and she was linked first to Anthony Cledis of the Red Hot Chilli Peppers, then Adam Duritz of the band Counting Crowes. She moved on to actors, notably Tate Donovan now of the OC, whom she dated for about three years, got engaged to and then split from before a certain Brad Pitt came along.

They were set up for their first date, a dinner date, in 1997 after which they became inseparable. They got married on July 29th 2000 at a super private and lavish ceremony in Malibu where guests had to pass through metal detectors amongst other security measures taken to keep out the press.

Everything seemed perfect for Jennifer about this time, Friends was going strong, her movies were doing great. She starred in a small independent movie, the 'Good Girl' opposite a then twenty year old Jake Gyllenhaal in her most dramatic role to date, which earned her an Independent Spirit Award nomination. She also starred opposite Jim Carrey in 'Bruce Almighty' which had huge box office returns, (it grossed over $100m in its first week of release). 'Along Came Polly' in which she starred with Ben Stiller was also a mega hit with audiences Worldwide. At the end of 2003 she topped the Forbes Most Powerful in Hollywood list. She went on to form 'Plan B Productions' with Brad Pitt and even said in an interview that "it was great to be doing all these things with Brad because you had your best bud by your side forever".

The only relationship in her life that had turned sour up to that point was with her Mother with whom she became estranged following the publication of a tell all type of book by Mummy. They later made up after several years of bitterness and acrimony.

Jennifer also got along very well with people in general as evidenced by the number of close personal friends she has in her life, Courtney Cox-Arquette being the closest of the lot.

They in turn (her best friends) have a lot of wonderfully nice things to say when describing her such as "one of the kindest, one of the most authentic, one of the most original and one of the most dignified etc, etc, people you will ever meet".

Lisa Kudrow a Friends cast- mate when asked about Jen in an interview said that she is an emotionally available person which made her perfect for a friend.

From all indications, life seemed great for Jennifer all round at about this time, then Brad went to begin shooting Mr. and Mrs. Smith which wrapped in September 2004. Jen's World fell apart, crumbled, shattered, disintegrated, imploded, (take your pick), very shortly there - after.

Mr. Bradley "Brad" William Pitt:

*B*rad Pitt was the eldest of three children born to a Mother who was a School Counselor and a Father who was an Executive in a Trucking Firm. He was born in Shawnee Oklahoma on December 18 1963. The family later moved to Springfield, Missouri. Brad attended the University of Missouri from 1982-1986 majoring in Journalism, yes JOURNALISM (the profession of Journalists which may or may not include members of the paparazzi, depending on who you talk to) and Advertising. He left College two credits short of graduation (hard to imagine) and headed for California.

He did odd jobs to pay for acting classes such as chauffeuring strippers around in a limousine and escorting them to bachelor parties (a stripper pimp), dressing in a chicken outfit outside a restaurant and was a refrigerator boy. His story was the usual, bit parts here and there or leads in bad movies until his breakout role in Thelma and Louis in 1991, which he had Billy Baldwin's conflicting employment in another movie to thank for the opportunity. Billy Baldwin was already cast in Thelma and Louis but had to drop out for a bigger role in 'Backdraft'. Brad had only fourteen minutes of film time but he made the most of it because he gave such a memorable performance that he has not looked back since. On the other hand where has Billy's career gone since 'Backdraft'. This sort of reminds us all that Rob Lowe also recently turned down the part of McDreamy on Grey's Anatomy ensuring that second choice Patrick Dempsey became the new toast of Tinsletown, yes C'est la vie indeed.

Brad was crowned People Magazine's Sexiest Man Alive twice, in 1995 and 2000 and named one of the 100 sexiest stars in film history in 1995 by another one of those Magazines. He has been nominated for an Oscar twice in the supporting actor category for his performances in the 'Fight Club' and 'Seven Monkeys' respectively.

He married actress, Jennifer Aniston in 2000 and was divorced from her in 2005. He immediately settled down with his Mr. and Mrs. Smith co-star Angelina Jolie and adopted her two children, a boy, Maddox (Cambodian origin) and a girl Zahara not Shakira (Ethiopian origin). They now have a baby girl named Shiloh delivered by Angelina in Namibia in May 2006.

The couple really appear to share a deep love of charity and have recently set up the Jolie-Pitt Foundation to fund their various charitable ventures mainly aimed at providing for deprived children Worldwide, very noble. Their joint commitment to this worthy Causes seems one hundred percent genuine and is highly commendable for sure.

Still on the topic of charity, it is pertinent to note here that those joining the band wagon purely for publicity as witnessed of late in the spate of celebrities mouthing off about their sudden love for Africa and all things African etc will surely be whittled down as rapidly as it began when their actions do not support their spoken words aimed solely at self aggrandizement only, shame on them.

The 'it' couple are also reportedly planning to embark on a space mission together by traveling in the new Virgin Galactic Commercial Space Travel shuttle to be launched in 2008.

Ms. Angelina "Ange"Jolie:

Angelina Jolie was born on 4 June 1975 to Oscar winning actor Jon Voight and a French Mother (Marcheline Betrand) who gave up her Career as an aspiring actress to raise Ange and her older brother James. Her Parents were separated when she was very young and she and James both lived with their Mother. It was widely reported that she had her first serious boyfriend when she was fourteen years old and he turned out to be a live-in boyfriend. Her Mother simply asked him to move him with them to be better able to monitor them or something of that nature. All I say to that is hmm.

She always knew she wanted to act and in those days in the beginning, her brother was her first coach and director. She was a loner as a child and it was around this time she discovered her passion for the darker side of life. She was interested in dead bodies and embalming and even considered becoming a funeral director. She also became fascinated with knives and blood. Apparently, she also engaged in self-mutilation and used to cut herself frequently.

She made up her mind quite early on the course her Career was going to take and at the age of 11 years she enrolled at the prestigious Lee Strasberg Theater Institute in New York. At the start of her Career she appeared in music videos for the likes of Lenny Kravitz and the Rolling Stones. She was a part time model and did some work on television, but her breakout role was for the HBO biopic movie "Gia" (about the life of the supermodel that died of aids in the 80"s). Her critically acclaimed performance in said movie earned her a golden globe award.

She followed this with an Oscar winning

performance in "Girl Interrupted" in 2000 .The joy of winning an Oscar was marred by the bad publicity that followed her acceptance speech where she declared that she was so in love with her brother right now and gave him a lingering kiss on the lips right there on the podium. Stories of an incestuous relationship soon trailed the pair and denials quickly followed. She then began to amass a reputation as a free spirited individual who always managed to fall for her male co-stars on every movie set.

Along the way, she also fell for a female co-star named Jenny Shimizu whom she met on the set of the film 'Foxfire' and told Barbara Walters in 2003 that she considers herself a very sexual person. She said **"If I fall in love with a woman tomorrow, it's right that I should want to kiss her and touch her"**. She was also later quoted as saying she would have loved to marry Jenny if same sex Marriage was legal at the time. Instead she married Jonny Lee Miller whom she had met in 1995 on the set of another film called 'Hackers' on March 28 1996.

The Marriage ceremony involved inscription of Jonny's name in blood on her blouse, with then struggling actor Jude Law acting as best man. She separated from him just over a year later. She later married Billy Bob Thornton in Las Vegas in May

2000 and yes you are right, they did meet on the set of a movie. She went on to describe him as her best friend whom she felt would always keep her safe from harm. She began to carry his blood around in a vile on her neck as a testament to her undying love for him. Can anyone forget the hugely famous "Billy Bob Forever" tattoo on the arm, which has since been painfully lasered off?

The two were never shy about their feelings and were always happy to tell anyone that would listen about their sexual antics usually ably supported with open displays of lust at various red carpet ceremonies. They even boasted about erecting strange structures in their home to further aid them in enjoying their favorite past time and could not understand why anyone would find this unusual or disturbing.

One recalls that Billy Bob also coincidentally played her husband in the movie that brought them together. Is it just I or does it seem as if a guy stands a very good chance of nabbing Ange once he plays her hubby in a film.

At the time Ange met Billy Bob, he was in a long-term relationship with actress Laura Dern who was later quoted as saying, after she found out about his Marriage to Angelina that: **"she went to shoot a movie and her boyfriend went and got married to**

someone else"

Not too long after her Marriage, Ange suddenly became very much interested in humanitarian work as a result of traveling for a movie shoot which exposed her to large scale human suffering. She became engrossed in the plights of the needy especially refugees and orphans. Around this period she was made a United Nations Goodwill Ambassador in recognition of her interest and efforts. She also became more vocal in seeking for assistance in the corridors of power and soon began to donate a large portion (a third) of her own income to these Causes.

Ange visited an Orphanage in Cambodia as part of her humanitarian work in 2001 and fell in love again, this time with a little boy whom she later adopted and named Maddox. Her Marriage to Billy Bob began to unravel and it all came to an end on the 3rd of June 2002 when Billy Bob walked out on her after a massive fight and she never saw him again. She filed for divorce later that year citing the most famous last words in Hollywood "irreconcilable differences".

At about the same time she fell out with her Dad who had expressed his concerns over her mental health and relationship choices publicly and in a published letter to her. She was very unhappy about this action from Daddy, which she felt could compromise her adoption plans for Maddox. Lets face it even a child in an Orphanage does not deserve to be with a psycho right? She got custody of Maddox whilst filming "Beyond Borders" in Africa in 2002. She then cut Daddy off and legally changed her last name from Voight to Jolie.

In spite of all the good she was doing and the seeming transformation in her life, Ange was still always linked with every male co-star in the new millennium that she worked with (from Val Kilmer to Ethan Hawke to Olivier Martinez to Colin Farrell, etc, etc), the list seemed endless and she did not do much to dispel all the rumors because she never did much to deny them, instead her utterances usually added fuel to the fire. In fact, it was reported in the media at the time that poor Kylie Minogue had to drop everything to rush off to Canada to be with Olivier when his friendship with Ange began to raise too many eyebrows on the set of the movie 'Taking Lives". It may just have been the case of Kylie missing Olivier though. Whatever it was, I am sure all Kylie fans are grateful today that Olivier's relationship with Kylie survived that trying period to enable him be with her at her time of deepest need for love and support, during her battle with breast cancer.

It got to the point where it seemed a bit shocking

to all keen observers but at the same time refreshing when British hunk, Clive Owen co-starred with her in 'Beyond Borders' and was obviously immune to her charms, because quite surprisingly or quite unpredictably his marriage was still intact after the movie.

Then Ange signed on for Mr. and Mrs. Smith to star opposite Brad Pitt in 2004 and as they always say, the rest is history or should I say, res ipsa loquitor. The conception of brand Brangelina had just taken place and the birth of the Jolie-Pitt's was just round the corner. Did you just suppress a yawn; I thought so.

During the denial frenzy, Ange could not resist directing a jab at her estranged Dad when she claimed she would never date a married man after seeing first hand the pain a similar action of being unfaithful on the part of her Dad caused her own Mother. We all know how hollow or shallow that sounded (coming from her), after events began to unfold between her and a certain Bradley, William Pitt soon thereafter.

Most Recognised Quote By Ange

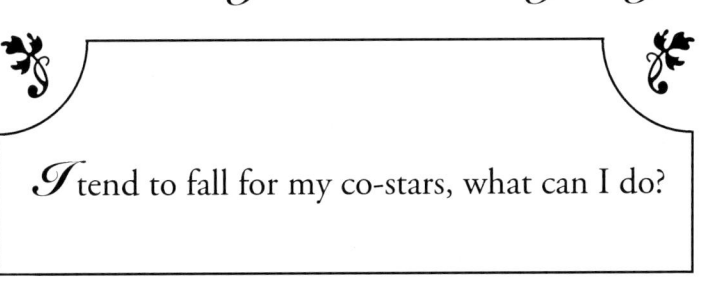

I tend to fall for my co-stars, what can I do?

2

The Marriage of Jennifer and Bradley: A Fairy Tale Turned Nightmare

How celebrated was this union? How well matched were they? The coming together of two beautiful people blessed with talent, good looks, charming personalities, successful Careers and huge bank accounts, what could possibly go wrong?

They met through the match making antics of their respective agents. It seemed they fell deeply in love. They took a long trip together visiting different parts of the World (sounds rather familiar), including the Middle East to help them determine the next step in their relationship.

When the impending wedding was announced it was not a surprise to anyone as some unions in Hollywood between two people sometimes is. In their case it was more a question of when and how and not why. By all accounts it, the wedding was a very nice affair, but one cannot help but wonder whether the lengths they went to and steps they took to ward off certain people with a penchant for taking pictures and spreading tales did not take a bit of the shine off.

All things considered every thing went well and a new "golden Marriage' excuse the pun, was thought to have been created in the land of fairy tales. It seemed like a match made in heaven. Their union went through the usual scrutiny. Where were they dining tonight? Where are they vacationing, in between movie shoots? When will their first bundle of joy arrive? Whose taste in furnishing was more prevalent in their new massive (emphasis on massive) mansion in Beverly Hills, since they were reportedly both known to favour vastly different architectural designs and artifacts, modern architecture for one and ancient European for the other.

By the way, that turned out to be the same massive mansion that was recently sold to the highest bidder before Brad and Jen ever actually lived in it, after it had just been completely refurbished and redecorated, (which apparently cost a fortune and took years of joint work and effort of both of them to transform the place), how sad is that!

As usual time spent apart was watched closely and the never-ending speculation about Jen's various alleged pregnancies or pregnant stages, came with the territory. Of course the denials always came from the couple's representatives. Even when Rachel became pregnant in Season 8 of Friends, Jen still did not take the bait. In retrospect Jennifer do you not agree that it should have been the perfect way to start a family? Were the producers trying to tell you something or were they trying to make it easy for you to make the expected announcement without worrying about whether it would be written into the script, who knows?

Actually, I think we all just expected to hear the good news eventually or at some point anyway, but it was going to be at their own pace, they were not going to be rushed into parenthood just because other people were calling for a baby. At least, that was how we expected their Marriage to progress, with the passage of time.

There was always speculation about Jen's show 'Friends' as well, would there be another season after the current one, how much more money (over one million dollars) can each of the friends get per episode. We were then told that the tenth season would be the last and everyone thought that the time for the pity patter of tiny feet was drawing ever closer for our favorite friend and her eye candy hubby; yes!

But, alas, that was not the case, it was not to be because suddenly all the headlines had a familiar theme: Should Jen be worried that Brad's new film project will star him opposite a certain Ms. Angelina Jolie. The plot of the new movie did not do much to allay fears of genuine supporters of the Brad and Jen union, because there were going to be steamy sex scenes between the pair. If you were looking for the meaning of 'danger' or 'trouble' in the dictionary, then it seemed that scenario would have aptly been a valid demonstration of either.

Yet others said no way, a man like Brad knows the value of what he has with Jen, he will not jeopardize that for an unstable fling no matter how enticing, They said Brad is smarter than we were all giving him credit for. Oh yes, the second-guessing had begun, although it seemed a bit unwarranted or hasty at the time. I mean, the shooting of the movie had not even commenced. Yes indeed, that old saying is true in this case that there is never any smoke without a fire.

Filming began on the set of Mr. and Mrs. Smith and immediately the rumors started almost simultaneously. You sensed palpable fear even in the media for Jennifer and Brad's union because it was becoming clear to some people around them at the time that Brad seemed to be more than willing to re-evaluate his life options, he was sending all the wrong signals for a happily married dude, but all the right signals for extra curricular activities.

We began to hear that Brad and Ange were getting on extremely very well, we heard that the on set chemistry was almost choking. They were holding hands all the time, they were poking each others bodily parts for laughs at every opportunity, they were even rumored to have passed on viruses to one another from too much kissing on the set, did I say virus, oh sorry must have been a 'slip of tongue'. Brad apparently even developed more interest in Maddox than Billy Bob ever did.

According to some reports, the little tot even started referring to Brad as 'Daddy' by the time shooting on the set of the movie wrapped, wow.

Alarm bells were ringing rather loudly for

Jennifer, poor woman. At that point what could she do? She could not demand for a script re write or review to delete all sex scenes, she could not disengage Brad from the project, it was way too late and even if it wasn't you somehow sensed that they did not have the sort of union where Jen would say to Brad – No ways are you going to be in a movie with Angelina Jolie. It seemed like she went out of her way to be supportive of his Career choices and was hopeful that their love and trust would prevail over temptation.

As it turned out, Jen was wrong on all counts whilst Brad just went along with the flow for as long as it was convenient for him to play along. This is extremely different from his present relationship where you sense that once Ange says No to something, anything at all, that would mean NO for Brad and that would be that about that!

As far as her support for Brad went, Jennifer also played unwittingly into Ange's hands (knowing her reputation), by stopping to say hi to her in the parking lot or somewhere like that (first meeting of the two) shortly before Mr. and Mrs. Smith began filming and saying to her innocently that her husband Brad was looking forward very much to working with Ange in their new movie. Talk about wetting the appetite of a man eater with a little bit too much information.

By the time Mr. and Mrs. Smith wrapped in September 2004, Jen was astonished to discover that her husband, the love of her life, the man she thought she was going to spend her remaining time on Earth with and who was going to be the Father of her children suddenly went missing and he seemed to be a totally different person. When 'Friends' was closing shop after ten years and his wife needed his support and understanding, he was no longer interested in providing it. He checked out emotionally from the Marriage and from all things Jennifer. Ange fever was on the rampage and Brad did not want to be cured.

In spite of the smokescreen party Brad hosted for Jen that gave hope of reconciliation shortly after the announcement, it was way too late. The Marriage was over. It had lasted just over four years and they had been together for seven years.

One is not privy to the tell tale signs that usually occur when one spouse is beginning to check out whilst the other is trying to hold on in this instant because both parties are a bit tight lipped. In Brad's case, keeping mum was key lest he became much more of a cad than we all originally imagined. It was not in his best interest to say anything at that time because from all indications he knew he was already involved in an extra marital affair or about to embark on one very shortly, so why say anything. As for Jen, she seemed to be in a daze for a while, not knowing who or what to believe about the real reasons her Marriage was no more.

For Brad his strategy appeared to be to play the child starved card and focus as much attention as possible on kids at every opportunity without actually calling out Jen on the issue, to try and win some sympathy whilst he was pre occupied with throwing some heavy swords into the back of his ex missus whose only crime was her unconditional love for her husband.

A typical example would be his interview on the red carpet at the premiere of 'Oceans 12', on the topic of kids, Brad was beaming when he told a reporter the following:

Brad Pitt Quotable Quote

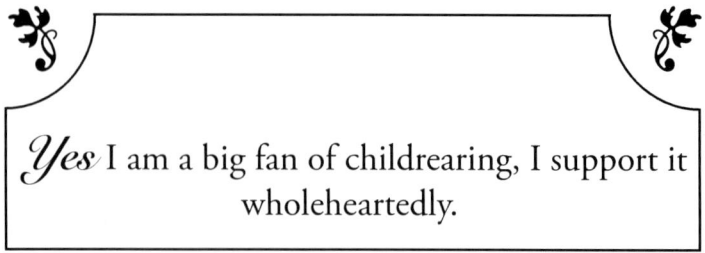

Yes I am a big fan of childrearing, I support it wholeheartedly.

3

A Comparative Analysis of Lifestyles and Upbringing

In a brief comparison of lifestyles, upbringing, exposure and education we see similarities and dis- similarities between the three principal parties. For example, only Brad's Parents still remain together as a married couple up until the present time. Both Jen and Ange's Fathers left home when they were quite young, Ange was much younger than Jen when her Father left her Mother.

Interestingly, we see a number of additional similarities between Brad's women. They have in common, the fact that both sets of Parents were in show business, actors/aspiring actors, with Ange's Dad Jon Voight being the most recognizable name in film, of the lot. Jen's Dad had a long run in the daytime soap 'Days of our Lives' in the eighties. Are you also thinking, eh yeah, kind of like ex fiancée Gwyneth Paltrow, whose late Dad was accomplished director, Bruce Paltrow and Mother is the one and only Blythe Danner. I guess Mr. Pitt set certain standards for himself regarding his women, the more successful he became.

The two women grew up in the show business communities of Los Angeles and New York. Brad on the other hand had a more conservative upbringing with Parents who held normal type jobs, maybe its not so surprising that their Marriage lasted after all.

Of the three, Brad was the only one that went to College, but the fact that he left two credits short of graduation was perhaps a pointer to his future lifestyle in relation to Marriage and Commitment.

Ange seemed to have the most liberal Mom of the three or of all time. I mean how many fourteen year olds do you know in the eighties that lived with their boyfriends at home in the same house as their

Mom at her own behest. I wonder how this freedom helped to shape Ange in terms of her sexuality and her seeming knack for getting any man she desires.

Of the three, Brad seemed to know how to seize the moment perfectly, he only featured in fourteen minutes of film time in Thelma and Louise and stole the show, with a large dose of help from those abs and long blond locks of course. Also, of the three, Jen was the least controversial, she always seemed to exude a sense of loyalty and dependability and self-confidence. Ange on the other hand was full of controversy relating to her male sexual conquests in general, some women, specifically a certain Jenny Schmizu, her relationship with her Dad, her own utterances about her sexuality and attitude to sex and even her seemingly abnormal closeness to her own brother. Her penchant for other people's blood did nothing to redeem her public perception. All of that of course gradually began to change for the better once Maddox entered the picture. The adoption of Zahara at the height of the Brangelina scoop saved the little girl's life but that did not stop the scratching of heads of course.

With regard to Brad, we all discovered at about the same time that he displayed a penchant for displaying his affection for the World to see by being in sync with his current significant other at the time, (the flavor of the month). This usually took the form of a new matching hair cut or hair do or change of hair color to the same as that of the main squeeze at the time.

In terms of looks, Ange was at her most unattractive when she was with Billy Bob Thornton. She definitely could not have won a lot of awards relating to good looks at this time. Her makeover coincided with her appointment by the UN and her adoption of Maddox so that by the time she began filming Mr. and Mrs. Smith she was smoking hot. Jen on the other hand was the most consistent of the lot with regard to looks and hair color etc.

Whilst Jen's attitude and behaviour has always been consistent, Ange suddenly found her reason for existing after she adopted Maddox. Her focus seemed to change to include a lot more humanitarian work, which involved traveling all over the world, particularly to Africa. Jen on the other hand kept her charitable ventures a bit more closely to her chest and did less traveling because of the time dedicated to her hit TV show and Brad, presumably.

Brad has since embraced everything Ange does with regard to charity work and has gone on to adopt Ange's two adopted children as well. You sense that the man can't get enough of Ange at this moment, lets just hope they are still together before this book goes to print, fingers crossed on that one.

They have all won acting awards for their various works, but Ange is leading in the most prestigious award category, an Oscar. In terms of tattoos and divorce petitions, Ange is leading both Brad and Jen as well.

A striking difference between the two women also has to do with friends (not the show) and friendship. Everywhere you look around Jen, she is surrounded by very close female friends, that surprisingly includes a lot of actresses. Surprising because acting is such a cutthroat business full of jealousy and backbiting. Ange on the other hand does not appear to the onlooker to thrive on female friendship except for Jenny what's her name of course.

However of late she may have decided to open up to a new female friend in the person of new Mom Gwen Stefani, good for her. I suppose one cannot blame any woman who does not want to be friends with Ange especially if they have a man. Who wants to be friends with someone you constantly have to monitor your boyfriend or husband with. You do not want to start interpreting or mis- interpreting even the most innocent of nuances and you definitely do not want to be friends with someone you cannot plan foursome trips with, without second guessing yourself and your actions and suffering from panic attacks wondering if you will still have your man at the end of the trip.

Whilst on the subject of possibilities what if you suddenly discover you are a lesbian after such a trip? This could be alarming or disarming depending on who made the discovery. For example, we would have to assume based on her own recent admission that someone like Ellen Pompeo of Grey's Anatomy might actually be esctatic about such a development.

It even seemed at some point that one's husband merely had to be in the same movie with Angelina and divorce soon followed whether Ange had something to do with it or not. That was certainly the case with Ethan Hawke and Uma Thurman after filming ended on the set of 'Taking Lives', although it turned out that the other woman was not even almost famous.

History Repeats

It is noteworthy to point out that Brad has now repeated or replicated for Jen what her Father did to her Mother when she was a child by leaving her for another woman thereby opening old wounds all over again and inflicting fresh hurt and pain. Bringing back insecurities of her childhood and fresh despair. All the feelings she had hoped never to experience in her own personal life as an adult have now been revisited. It will definitely take a Herculean effort for her to expose herself like that to another man again and be trusting of men in general, in the future.

After all is said and done, I doubt that anyone is surprised at Brad's Mom's reported apparent reluctance to severe ties with her son's ex wife. All things considered, the woman has every right to be wary, her maternal instincts are at red alert, alarm bells must be ringing loud in her head even if she tries to forget all she has learned of Ange's past in spite of all the good deeds she is now doing. Particularly since she knows very well like the rest of the World does that holier than thou acts or not, Ange is the only reason why her son's Marriage collapsed.

If the reports are also true that she does not seem to see eye to eye with Ange at the moment on anything at all, it only serves to keep us all guessing frantically. I mean is it imaginable that Brad and Jen can still get back together after all that has transpired?

4

Brangelina is Born

*O*nce we started hearing and reading the rumors about all the physics, chemistry and biology going on between the main stars of Mr. and Mrs. Smith, even before the separation of Brad and Jen, it was time for a massive coronary type holding of collective breaths across the Universe.

Suddenly some of those whispers became louder, like oh no Brad should know better, others said why did Jennifer ever let him go near her, as if Brad was a baby that must be chaperoned all over the place.

Not a few people said Ange has a new image now, surely she would not be party to the wrecking of a beloved union such as this one was thought to be. Other people also noted that the Marriage of Brad and Jen was so strong that even Ange could not make a dent in it, etc,etc,etc.

Then we all saw the spread in 'W' Magazine with Brad, Ange and the little kids in various poses depicting a close-knit family. It turned out that Brad also owned the publishing rights to that publication. This was the action that led Jennifer to later question whether Brad was missing a sensitivity chip Alas it was dawning on everyone at the same time that every single rumor about the pair had a basis after all.

The Magazine spread appeared to be saying to Jen (albeit indirectly) that although she did not have kids for Brad, he intended to rectify that situation soon by having several with his new girlfriend. The pictures did all the talking that was necessary in the circumstances. By this time, a lot of people had started jumping on the infant bandwagon. People said different things; most agreed that maybe Jennifer should not have starved him of kids when she knew how much he wanted them.

We were informed that he had especially wanted

a little girl that looked like Jennifer precisely, to make his life complete. A certain headline grabbing housewife even gladly wore a T-Shirt, with: **"I'll have your baby, Brad,"** printed boldly on it. How heartless are those of Hollywood ilk, one ponders. No doubt Brad was secretly amused and pleased at the diversion. But spare a thought for Jennifer who was still trying to deal with an unraveled Marriage and still trying to accept the fact that her man flew with supersonic or dare I say, Concorde like speed into the arms of someone else, a femme fatale no less, if all the stories she was hearing were true.

On their part, Brad and Ange and their representatives denied and denied and denied some more. The denials related to any talk of an affair between the two. They even pretended not to acknowledge the presence of one another at the premiere of Mr. and Mrs. Smith in the U.S.A even though we heard that Brad was in Ange's hotel room earlier in the day picking out clothes and jewelry for her for the premiere. Ange also came out with some muddled garb about not ever dating a married man because of the scars left during her childhood by what her Daddy had done to her Mummy when he was unfaithful, yeah right. In the midst of all the denials, more pictures, this time of the new family vacationing in Africa, Kenya to be exact (a sign of things to come out of Namibia in future).

With all that was going on people would not stop talking about baby this and baby that. They tried to apportion blame proportionately because people felt that Brad could not have left Jen for Ange just like that. There had to be a very valid reason that made him give up on his Marriage. On and on it went. There seemed to be nowhere to hide for Jennifer, paparazzi wanted to see how she was coping. It was enough to send anyone into rehab and I bet Jen was no exception. To make matters worse, imagine her having to promote a film titled 'The Breakup' not too long afterwards.

It must have seemed like a hammer blow to the oesophagus for Jennifer and unfortunately for her instead of the pain easing up after appropriate medication, this pain would not be allowed to go away anytime soon because some people exist to make her realize everyday of her life, at every opportunity never missed to let her know that her husband left her for the sexiest, most luscious, most beautiful, most smoldering hot human being (not just woman) on the planet. Some individuals in the media for example those at the 'E' Entertainment Network have gone as far as to declare that her looks defy Earthy descriptions, that she is the most genetically gifted individual created by God so far, that it is an insult to equate her with mere mortals on this planet because her beauty simply defies logic and commonsense, they have come to the conclusion that Angelina Jolie is sui generis.

It would be remise of me if I were to fail to mention here that it was rather refreshing to discover recently that not all men over there find her attractive, thanks to remarks made by the rather quarrelsome Donald Trump.

They, the media, or more specifically the E Network, surprisingly acknowledge that though she was also created by God, that he was in a most pleasant, jovial and happy mood on the day in question. What can I say; I mean it appears some people have gone completely insane. Is this the same Hollywood with drop dead gorgeous beauties like Nicole Kidman, Eva Mendes, Ashley Judd, Jessica Alba, Scarlett Johansson, Kate Beckinsale and Charlize Theron, I wonder?

They even go as far as to suggest that by means of adoption she has been able to bestow her genes on these children such that the kids are also receiving best looking awards all over the place, amazing. The question that comes to mind sometimes is this: Does anyone look at Jon Voight and remember Ange is a part of him? (She does bear a striking resemblance to her Daddy, after all). Why does he not receive any accolades for his looks or genes and stuff like that, er, just a thought.

5

A Closer Look at Team Brangelina, ("The Jolie-Pitts")

A lot can be said for the couple of the moment at this moment in time. They appear somewhat compatible at least in the looks category, not that Brad was not compatible with Jen looks wise, but sometimes one must still state the obvious, that's all.

It seems fair to say that of Brad's ex girlfriends, the one he was least compatible with in terms of looks was the talented actress, Juliette Lewis and as for Robin Givens, it would have been impossible to achieve that type of compatibility anyway. That probably explains why he never tried to color his face black or brown at any time for Robin's sake.

Brad and Ange seem to be at the same place in their lives, on the same page as they say, wanting similar things, raising kids, adopting kids, doing charity work, piloting small planes and traveling the World with emphasis on the words 'World' and 'Travel'. They also shared a serious penchant for dating their co-stars generally, with Jennifer Aniston being one of the few exceptions in Brad's case, as they did not meet on a movie set.

They are also suffering from a case of cold feet simultaneously which is not in the least surprising. Apparently if the Entertainment Networks are to be believed, they are also hoping to keep their relationship infidelity proof by each promising to avoid steamy sex scenes in future projects. This should prove really useful, as they both know too well. Although we are now hearing that Ange cannot wait to lock lips with a woman in a movie scene as soon as possible, because she enjoys it so much, sorry Brad.

However, they might need to expand that pledge

of theirs to include working with any actors or actresses that are remotely hot and interaction with all humans above the age of twenty and below the age of seventy, period.

On a lighter note, should the very talented Ms.Cate Blanchett be feeling very unattractive or what? I ask this question because she will reportedly be starring opposite Brad Pitt in more than one movie in quick succession, which by implication suggests that Ange is not that worried to unleash Brad on her frequently.

For example, I strongly suspect that we will not be seeing Brad Pitt in a movie with Scarlett Johansson anytime soon, at least whilst he and Ange are still together.

The areas of possible strain on the relationship all point towards Ange at the moment. This is because she seems to be less yielding than Brad on most of the issues that have come up in the relationship. Everything seems tilted too much in her favor at this time, and it appears as if Brad is still pinching himself and not yet fully awake.

A typical scenario that may lead to a case of rude awakening for Mr. Pitt is that of the exes. The ex in question is Jonny Lee Miller, Ange's first husband, certainly not the more familiar Billy Bob who performed a vanishing act on the eve of his wife's 27th birthday. If the latest news is to be believed, Ange is refusing to stop calling and communicating with Jonny. She recently employed him to help film a documentary and he has even confessed that there is still a lot of love between them. We have been told that Brad on the other hand has gone out of his way to please her as usual, by cutting off all ties with Jen, gifting Ange, Jen's rumored potential role in the Daniel Pearl movie and even instructing his Mom to end her relationship with Jen.

This should be worrisome if you are Brad because Ms. Jolie had once confessed that the most stupid thing she ever did in her life was to divorce Jonny. There were also reports that at the time she was enjoying the attentions of her Alexander co-star, Mr. Farrell, she still found time (a lot of it) for Jonny, during that period. One wonders if the enduring love between the ex couple still carries a sexual undertone or whether it is a brother/sister type of love. In Angelina Jolie's case, either one cannot be too reassuring for Mr. Pitt. I mean how many sisters do you know who are giddy about buying matching bondage cuffs with their own brother? I personally do not know a single one, but that's just me.

The icing on the cake, depending on whose cake

it is, is that Jonny who is British is reportedly moving to Hollywood (nearer Ange) shortly, because a pilot he is involved with has been picked up by one of the Networks (ABC). That is a developing situation that needs to be monitored closely and only Mr. Pitt might not be so amused about it at all. This may turn out to be one case where what is good for the goose is definitely not good for the gander. We'll have to wait and see

Another issue that may impact on the relationship is that of normalcy. They seem to be going to extra ordinary lengths to achieve ordinary things. How long before someone cracks. Case in point, if the daily ten people (Ange's BFF's) are to be believed then she recently requested for an all female service at a high brow eatery recently because she is getting tired of men gawking at her. If this is true then she is obviously beginning to believe all the hype about her looks. I mean how much gawking can go on whilst you are being served dinner by professionals, maybe she's been unlucky enough to be served by part timers (mostly students) on a regular basis. Something is off about that request anyhow.

Also traveling all the way to Namibia to have their baby reportedly cost just over Two Million United States Dollars in accommodation bills alone.

We were informed that the cost of private jet hire for one leg of the trip cost about $250,000. Add to these security costs, we all remember the lengths the Namibian Government went to protect Brangelina, leading to arrests in some cases. Correct me if I am wrong but this strikes me as the most expensive birth in history without a doubt. Definitely one for the record books. Going to such lengths to please Ms. Jolie may take its toll sooner or later. And to think we all labeled Ms. Jennifer Lopez a diva, sorry J.lo.

In far away India of late, we have seen pictures of one of their bodyguards practicing a very dangerous chokehold on a photographer around the neck to prevent him from taking pictures. A car belonging to the Brangelina fleet also struck a teenager who was on a bicycle, whilst attempting to flee the paparazzi, luckily the young man was unhurt. The Indian Government had to deploy more security to protect the famous couple; these were probably officers that may have served the Indian people better in a lot of other capacities. There are also reports of people pretending to be in the employment of the United States Secret Service for the sole reason of being contracted to protect Brangelina. When a couple is beginning to require security that may be almost at par with George W. Bush, certainly more than the Presidents of some other Countries and Royalty even, it all just makes you wonder how they can ever lead a normal life.

A potential flashpoint could be the employment of Nannies for their growing brood. The age of Nannies and their number as well as their looks might be a source of concern to both parties in this relationship. I mean, what if they both fall for the same Nanny? A mundane task such as appointment of Nannies may take on an extra dimension, as they have to be scrutinized more carefully than normal, in the Jolie-Pitt household. The older the better rule may be silently employed. Again, we'll have to wait and see.

Also, it is not clear what Brad's dear relative (Grandma, to be precise), meant recently when she implied that Brad was still hurt from the end of his Marriage to Jennifer and so is not in a hurry to marry Ange until he is certain he can keep his promise of together forever, this time. You know the same Grandma that was quoted by In Touch Magazine at the beginning of their relationship to have said: **" I know who Angelina Jolie is and that she has a child, but I think it's a shame that she is his new girlfriend, its all very disturbing".**

With that type of statement credited to her, you

just suspect that she will not be welcome in any new home Ange is creating with Brad. She will definitely not be on her Christmas shopping list unless that type of treatment is reserved exclusively for Mr. Voight only, of course. Wonder how the new "Mr. Jolie" will handle this very delicate situation involving two people he obviously cares deeply about, if indeed it arises.

On the issue of hurting and being hurt as his Grandma now suggests, how can Brad be hurt by the end of his Marriage when he ended it? Yes, Jen filed for divorce, but it was at Brad's request or at the very least, his very own device or design depending on individual interpretation of his conduct at the time his Marriage ended. Since then "he has gotten all that he ever wanted out of life". Why is he still hurting? Or why was he hurt at all? All rather strange, maybe someone is trying to pool the wool over our probing eyes.

Methinks however that Mr. Pitt may slowly be discovering that it might be foolhardy to commit to Ange in that manner seeing as he hardly seems to be getting any words in on anything for now. Of course, there is also a School of thought that strongly believes Ange is the one holding out because she is not trying to beat Elizabeth Taylor's record, she does not even want to compete with Jennifer Lopez in the number of husbands category, if she can avoid it and she is currently trying her best.

The most pertinent issue in the Jolie-Pitt relationship may be that of trust. No matter how hot and heavy the couple is right now, it is only natural for both parties to be harboring some degree of mis-trust for one another. On Ange's part, mis-trust of Brad will be in her subconscious because if he can turn on Jen and dump her so abruptly the way he did, because he took a fancy to another woman albeit herself, this must make her think from time to time: What's to stop him doing the same to me tomorrow? Already we are hearing rumblings relating to Ange's suspicions regarding Brad's faithfulness, apparently because he is becoming emotionally distant of late. Is there anyone else out there thinking wow that's rather predictable.

The answer to the mis-trust issue if any, may lie in the children of the union, even if Brad gets fed up with Ange at some point, highly unlikely from all indications, those kids will invariably tie him to her much longer than anything else can. For that reason one must admit that Ange was way smarter than Jen in recognizing what needed to be done to keep a self confessed drifter in line and on board. I mean how fast did she get pregnant, certainly seemed as if it happened with lightning speed.

On Brad's part because Angelina Jolie is Angelina Jolie, she is who she is, he is bound to wonder occasionally if it is really possible for her to suddenly change one hundred percent and become devoted to one person, him.

On the issue of Marriage between the two, Brad recently stated in interviews that Ange and he will wed only if Marriage is allowed (legalized) for everyone in America that wishes to engage in it. It seems this couple will do anything to score cheap PR points for themselves, what hog wash, utter nonsense.

Whatever the reasons for their reluctance to tie the knot however, it may yet prove to be the best thing they ever did or not do together in this most intriguing of relationships.

Of the two, it seems fairly obvious to say that Ange would have to be declared stark raving mad or a looney (as some have argued in the past), to leave Brad or do anything to jeopardize the relationship to any grave degree. This is simply because of what she has gained as a result, a man who is ready to do anything she wants, did I say a man, oh my apologies, I meant to say an Arabian Stud, a Greek Adonis, Constant Contender for Sexiest Man Alive, the Hollywood version of Father Christmas to some degree, ready to spend any amount on her, who allows her to do whatever she deems fit including as widely reported in the media, flying small planes in the late stages of her pregnancy, (I mean the child is his as well, should he not have been more firm) especially when one examines what just happened to the Yankee Pitcher (Cory Lidle) that lost his life after his small plane flew into an apartment block in Manhattan and we are told that he was one of the most careful and prepared human beings (not known to be careless at all), in his lifetime. It makes you realize even if you did not do so before that piloting small planes especially with an unborn child in the later stages of a pregnancy is a little foolhardy at the very least.

At the risk of repetition, it seems clear that Brad will do anything and everything for Ange at this point in their relationship. It only remains to be seen if this will start reflecting on his body parts at some point. What if she wants his nose to be longer or his lips fatter or his eyes thinner (and what about those tattoos), or whatever else she comes up with, again we will have to wait and see.

From observing her demeanor whenever they are together, Ange appears to be genuinely in love with Brad just as much as he is with her, How hard can that be, really, or to borrow a Grey's Anatomy favorite, "seriously". So there may be no cause for alarm after all. Certainly, this is one relationship that will never fail to fascinate us all, whether we hate them or love them.

Reports had indicated that another potential Brangelina adoption is in the works. This time, an Indian child because they were filming in that Country. But baby Shiloh is not yet a year old right? If this adoption rumors are true like most of the other rumors about team Brangelina have turned out to be then some may argue that Shiloh's young age does not really matter because what of Parents of twins or triplets, those kids all come at the same time. Usually, they come most often to Parents that can ill afford them unlike in this case where there is an abundance of wealth and riches.

I beg to disagree with that argument though. My point of view comes from being one of six children and also being a mother of two young children who is trying her best to be as loving, diligent and hands on as is humanly possible with them. It is definitely not the easiest of jobs especially when they are at that very young age from day 1 to about eight years old. I have been told it gets easier when they are nearing ten years and upwards, who knows for sure.

One is likely to believe the latest adoption rumor or to believe that they may at the very least be working on another one for the near future because they have stated themselves in interviews that they want a house full of kids i.e. as much as a football team or perhaps even more, with Brad saying in interviews on more than one occasion that they would like to have enough children to start their own Country and dominate the Soccer World Cup, presumably after joining FIFA of course. All truly wonderful, but in their own case, that old saying (you know the one) about being careful what you wish for ...." may turn out to be spot on.

I mean, its okay or even very lovely to adore children and start adopting them in droves because your milk of human kindness is overflowing and all that but when it comes to children, to borrow from Brangelina's genre, filmography, I defer to the very eloquent words of that most intelligent of individuals to ever grace our screens, 'Forest Gump' when he says "life (for our purpose I'll say children) are like a box of chocolates, you never know what you are gonna get".

You can have one biological child and lavish him or her with love, gifts, a great education and all the good things in life and they can still turn out the opposite of what you expected, whereas you may adopt a child and do all those same things for them and they turn out perfect. I mean, just look at someone like Faith Hill who was adopted when she was three days old, is she not as close to perfection as any human being can be, I certainly think so, (whether she is a sore loser or not is another matter entirely).

However if you end up with twelve or so kids from different cultures, ethnicities, and varied emotional, psychological, health and medical heritages the stakes become higher, the odds are worsened, the chances of a couple of them not turning out according to the script of life carefully written out for them by you are more enhanced, not for any other reason but that it is what it is. Soon Yi, current wife to Woody Allen would be a perfect illustration of the point being made here, at least as far as Mia Farrow (her adoptive mother) is concerned.

When you have a house full of kids such as those from backgrounds described above and you also happen to be mega movie stars actively engaged in the business of movie making in addition to working for the United Nations to help save the World, which as the job description suggests involves traveling the World fairly frequently. What time are you likely to have for those dozen or so kids, especially as we all know that each one deserves as much quality time as the next.

Are the kids going to be raised mainly by expensive nannies? Will they have to change Schools every term due to all the traveling? Or, will they start attending Boarding School's from an early age? If the answers are mostly yes, you have to wonder whether their Parents have done them a great service or disservice?

In the long run, would it not have been better to pull an Oprah (yes, the one that's good friends with that Jennifer, which explains why we are unlikely to see Brangelina on that show ever), by building a wonderful, modern boarding pre-school or any other age relevant school for them in their various Countries to better equip them in life. Something that may also come up later amongst the kids has to do with hormones and feelings. What if Maddox develops a crush on Shiloh or Pax has feelings for Zahara? Going by their Mom's past history of extreme closeness to her own brother which raised a lot of eyebrows at one time and resulted in them becoming less affectionate in public, it would indeed be very interesting to witness. It is worth pointing out however that in Ange's situation with James, incest was never really established to have ever occurred although they did their best to make us all think otherwise. In the scenario painted above, incest in the strictest sense would not even apply, but it would be interesting to see how Mummy deals with such matters. Would she be encouraging, indifferent or displeased? Only time will tell. As for Brad it is hard to tell what his reaction will be because since hooking up with Ange he has given the impression to many that he no longer has a mind of his own.

Only time will tell in Brangelina's case because it will certainly get more interesting when those children start becoming adults and they are in a position to write tell all books. These are certainly not the interesting times for Brangelina, that's way in the future, say fifteen or so odd years from now. Raising children boils down to a gamble, it is however a gamble they are willing to take and no one should knock them for this, I guess. In the meantime, Grandma Betty may need to have another quick whisper in her grandson's ear.

I somehow sense that the majority of the dozen or so children Brangelina are planning on having will surely be adopted. I do not see Ange as the pregnancy happy type. Maybe it's just me again, but haven't you all noticed that Ange seems to have aged about ten years since the birth of baby Shiloh. I am not talking about baby fat, they all shed those pretty quickly nowadays and she has too. I am speaking of Ange from neck upwards; she just seems a lot older than she did at the height of Mr. and Mrs. Smith. Not when she's all made up for those commercials and all that publicity stuff obviously, (even I may pass for a beauty queen with all that make up on my face), rather I am referring to those occasions when she chooses to wear less make up on the humanitarian front or during those walks. I do not know if it's to do with having a baby which sometimes affects some women that way or whether its to do with the stress of life with Brad, how can it be that, right. Whatever the case, Ange is looking very un Ange like in a lot of sightings of late, in my humble opinion.

She has since blossomed a little just in time for the awards Season but we all know the herculean effort it takes from dozens of very well paid individuals in order for people like her to walk the walk on those red carpets.

Still on the subject of their deep love for kids, even Brangelina may have outdone themselves in far away India. Apparently they decided that it would be best to shoot a police station scene (for the movie about Danny Pearl currently being filmed in India instead of Pakistan), in a children's school on a school day without expecting the Parents to ever show up to pick up their kids. One must acknowledge that whomever decided on that location (love of children or not) must be a genius because only a select few would have thought of a school in session as an ideal replacement for a police station or for any other scene(s) for that matter for the purpose of a movie shoot.

Of course the Parents showed up as they always do and your guess is as good as mine as to what happened afterwards. We were then informed that in the melee that ensued even the children that Brangelina love so much were not spared from rough treatment by their guest's bodyguards along with their Parents. The bodyguards also reportedly issued some racial slurs in the process of carrying out their enviable task. The whole episode resulted in three of those bodyguards being arrested and released on bail. Brangelina then released separate statements supporting their employees, very noble indeed.

If I were one of their advisers however (the chances of Oprah becoming President are higher than this ever happening for sure), but just in case, I would advise them to pay more attention to the three individuals in question because this is a case of he said, she said. One is tempted to ask why would these everyday (ordinary) people say they heard racial slurs from those bodyguards if they were never uttered. What if those Parents were telling the truth and Brangelina have some bigots in their employ? This is important because if their own bodyguards are harboring such feelings towards 'indians' how can they be expected to 'adequately protect' Maddox (Cambodian) and Zahara (Ethiopian) both of whom they are also employed to protect, if and when push comes to shove?

Having said all that I have in this Chapter, something else that should help team Brangelina pull together is the negativity oozing from people like me in general. Although we are in the minority, the fact of the matter is that people in such a situation tend to try even harder to prove the doubters wrong about so many things none more so than the duration and durability of their relationship, fair wear and tear excepted of course, if for no other reason than to show those 'idiots' how stupid they are. It seems the child card is already yielding dividends for Ange in particular because it is now being reported that Brangelina have chosen to visit a Relationship Counselor to help them with their major differences of late instead of parting ways which would have been the more likely scenario were children not involved.

6

My Spouse, A Stranger

*E*verywhere in the world, spouses are waking up to stranger's everyday, it is a more common occurrence than most people think. It can manifest in different forms, such as behavioral tendencies, mannerisms or non-disclosure of material facts to mention a few. For example, a new wife who suddenly discovers that her husband is more frugal than he ever led her to believe whilst they were dating because he is now refusing to put money down for a dryer even though they got a washing machine as a wedding gift from his in laws.

Or, you suddenly discover your spouse cannot stand any member of your family, he was pretending all along. How many women would marry a man if they knew that after having his baby after induced labor (excruciatingly painful), he will show up and tell them to carry both the luggage and the baby out of the hospital whilst he strolls along unfettered?

What of a husband that has no qualms whatsoever in constantly exposing his young daughters to potential child abuse by paedophiles and also sees nothing wrong in offering a one year old alcohol? Or what about the one who is more fanatical about sports than he let on during the courtship and is now no longer interested in any outing unrelated to sports? Or one that suddenly stops taking you out to eat once you are married to him and only orders take out for himself and his friends when they visit without even ordering anything for the wife?

There are cases of spouses that appeared to merely be social drinkers, and then they start drinking themselves into a stupor at every opportunity, after the wedding. There are a lot of people especially women that will testify to this as a regular occurrence in their lives.

What of a husband that is always very happy

to go out of town for weekends with his barber (male) for fishing or whatever else they get up to and never shows any enthusiasm whatsoever about accompanying his wife anywhere. Nowadays, it is becoming a familiar storyline to discover that one spouse has just confessed to being gay on national television.

There are also situations where spouses discover that their partners have secret children that they never mentioned, until something happens to trigger the truth. In all these cases, a decision on what to do is made in the course of the Marriage. Dedicated Oprah viewers like myself know a thing or two about surprise revelations.

What happens when your spouse who was always attentive develops attention deficit disorder, eyes suddenly become shifty, his or her mind now always wondering, the telephone becomes the most important tool in life and all of a sudden work has made them too tired to even contemplate making love to you anytime soon.

What does one do in cases of such nature, when your spouse is no longer recognizable to you because of their conduct? Do you start to second-guess yourself or your spouse? Some questions are bound to occur and re-occur in the mind such as: Were you that stupid? How did you miss all the signs? Does your spouse have a split personality that is well hidden? Did your spouse ever love you at all? Why did you fall in love with such a person? Why did they ever come into your life?

All the above examples must be distinguished from a Nick and Jessica (the Newlyweds), scenario because the two of them did not seem to have much in common except maybe music. It was hard to tell whether they even liked the same kind of music. It was certainly not a case of Jessica pretending to be a football fanatic in order to get Nick to marry her, she did not care too much for sports, Nick on the other hand is crazy about sports.

You sense though that these two not being together any longer did not have too much to do with love of sports or lack of it. There were certainly more deep-rooted problems between the pair. The question will always remain however, couldn't they work it out somehow? I guess the answer is No, not in Hollywood, never!

Still on Jessica, I wonder whether her advisers were still in the womb when Usher's 'Confessions' Album was launched and sold over a million copies in its first week of release. Dear Jessica, your latest album is selling very poorly because the timing and message of your album was way off. You should have recognized the fact that people don't want to know how well you are doing post Nick, they want to know how much you are suffering and how ready you are to tear off Ms. "gold digger" Minnilo's hair extensions and shove them down her throat.

As for Nick, who keeps saying that he regrets agreeing to the 'Newlyweds' show on MTV? He needs to get a grip on reality because if not for that show, he will still be selling 35,000 records or less instead of over 500,000 that his new album has sold so far.

With regard to Jennifer Aniston however, one suspects that she only discovered she was married to a stranger (Brad Pitt) after the fact, (after the Marriage was over). She truly loved her husband and it seemed it was hard for her to believe that this new Brad doing all these mean things was the same Brad, the one she fell in love with and married. We all remember when she gushed in an interview that she fell in love with him because of his eyes, his soul and his heart. What happened to that Brad? Was the new Brad hiding deep inside the old one all along?

Discovering the new Brad along with all of America and the rest of the World must have been a rude shock to Jen. All of a sudden Brad wants to save all the children in despair, he is planning to have a house full of children, (his own football team), Brad wants to adopt children of all races, we discover that Brad may be nursing an ambition to work for the United Nations as a Goodwill Ambassador, Brad wants to single handedly save the environment, Brad had a sudden insatiable craving for jet setting and non stop flying, (in private jets and small planes), above all else, we happily noted that Brad had a deep love for the Continent of Africa, particularly the tiny nation of Namibia in South Africa. Who knew!

Imagine you are Jennifer and you now see Brad carrying kids in every single picture, every day over a period of say three months, you are bound to ask yourself what is the sudden obsession with kids, they existed prior to Mr. and Mrs. Smith did they not?

Don't get me wrong, its great for a man to love kids and show it (except Michael Jackson, of course) but you begin to wonder if he was deprived of the various opportunities to get kids before now, or what.

Also, imagine prior to his adoption of Angelina's kids, how Brad seemed to look more and more like a Manny (male nanny) ala Britney Spears style. Everywhere we saw Brad, (pictures of course) he was always carrying Zahara or leading Maddox along or riding a tricycle with both kids together, always wearing a diaper bag with a sheepish sort of grin firmly planted in place.

Whilst all the baby carrying painted a very pretty picture, it still left some scratching their heads even leading to headlines in some South African Magazines proclaiming that even Brad himself confessed to pals that he feels like laughing stock (a huge joke) and is unhappy that Ange has refused to employ more help for the kids. The answer to that may not be too far fetched, a certain Mr. Jude Law (one time best man at Ange's first wedding) may have inadvertently contributed to that decision by Ange unwittingly, we all still remember Nannygate of course.

By the time it dawned on us that Brad was beginning to look a little bit more like Ange, (albeit a more haggard version), he dyed his hair the same color as hers, the shock element had begun to wear off. It even brought back memories of the matching blond haircut he shared with then girlfriend Gwyneth Paltrow.

This brings me to the burning issues raised by the 'new' Brad's actions. Yes, its great to have kids, yes its great to adopt kids but are you not supposed to do those things with your spouse? Must you actually divorce your wife in order to develop a sudden penchant for children? The reason I say this is that if one believes Jennifer, children were not a source of discontent or disagreement in their Marriage because this was always part of their plans. Also, it did not seem so urgent or pressing to Brad at the time as it now appears to be.

Having said that however, Jen still has a lot of convincing to do in some quarters not that it matters anymore of course, since it is now a moot point. Reason being that it is very unusual for a young virile couple like Brad and Jen to be together for as long as seven years without at least one offspring to show for it, with the exception of Hilary Swank and Chad Lowe of course.

Unless there were fertility issues affecting Brad and or Jen one way or the other during the Marriage, you know like J.Lo eating tons of spinach on Doctors orders to help improve her fertility, that sort of thing. In the absence of any such problem on the part of either and with the true life evidence of baby Shiloh whom we all agree (without any evidence to the contrary) belongs to Brad then it becomes more believable that Jen is the one probably not as crazy about kids and having them as she would have us all believe. This is all speculation of course.

Are we then left with no choice but to believe that Brad felt there was no chance (zero, nil), of having kids or adopting kids with Jen. Why did he suddenly develop the paternal urge with someone else? What happened to till death us do part and all the other vows they shared? One gets the impression that the Marriage meant very little to Brad, we i.e. the public placed more premium on the Marriage than the principal actor did. He just packed up and left as soon as he found someone else he was attracted to.

Instead of Jen having Brad's babies or adopting babies with him, she has become an onlooker like all of us watching the drama unfold. In an ironic twist, she is now watching another actress play the part of Jennifer Aniston (how art sometimes imitates life). One part of the script that would definitely have had to change is the decision to have their child in Namibia. We all could never have imagined that Brad and Jen would have flown all the way to Namibia for the birth of their first child, how different things have become. Not that there is anything wrong with babies born in Africa, in actual fact some may argue that their baby may have been blessed with more brains and athleticism (African traits), as a result of her place of birth, debatable of course. Lets hope they return to Africa for their second child, why not.

Wait a minute, are we all not going a bit overboard with this baby issue anyways, you know this is the same Hollywood where a wife bears 5, yes FIVE children for a man and he still ends up impregnating Scary Spice, subject to DNA confirmation of course.

Reports have also indicated that Brad has enrolled for flying lessons so as to keep up with Ange who recently got her license, apparently, she is a big fan of piloting small planes.

If everything is taken into consideration as it relates to the pair, what has become most obvious to everyone is that surprisingly, Brad seems to be playing the role of the Missus in this relationship. I may be wrong but it seems as if the party with the balls in this relationship is also arguably the sexier of the two, at least she was at the beginning of the relationship, but of late, after another visit by Brad to the Salon, am not so sure. anymore.

As I stated before, television reports also indicated that Ange even flew a plane late into her pregnancy and it was ok with Brad not to mention the flier miles accumulated throughout her term albeit for very noble causes. It appeared to an onlooker as if what Ange wants, Ange gets (Brad just seemed to tag along) and of course Brad wants Ange, her kids and whatever Ange wants, not so bad for Ange, I guess.

It makes you wonder what would happen in that household if Shiloh suddenly develops a fascination with blood and knives.

Jennifer watched Brad whom she had once described as a goofy type of guy, a goody two shoes, who regularly opened car doors for her and was always a perfect gentleman towards her whilst they were together, suddenly become abundantly eager to inflict hurt and pain upon her tirelessly.

The latest icing on the cake for Ange or perhaps the latest dagger in the heart for Jennifer we have now been informed was indirectly inflicted by a company Jennifer herself collaborated with Brad to set up for their future, called Plan B Productions. Brad got the Production Company as part of the divorce settlement.

Well, Brad in his capacity as sole or majority stakeholder of Plan B has now employed guess who, yes you are right, he has employed Ms. Jolie to play the part of Marianne Pearl, the wife of Danny Pearl, the Wall Street journalist killed in Pakistan in an adaptation of Marianne Pearl's Memoir titled: "A Mighty Heart: The Brave Life and Death Of My husband Danny Pearl."

On the face of it there is nothing wrong with this, after all Ms. Jolie is an Oscar winning actress, however it has been widely reported that Jennifer herself was to have played the part of Marianne if not for the divorce, and had been hoping that this was the role that would have earned her, her first Oscar nomination. Further reports claim that it was Jen who convinced Marianne to accept Plan B's proposal for the upcoming project when she was expressing some reservations about pitching tents with them.

What is worthy of note here is that Plan B Productions seems a bit too self involved by all accounts because neither Jen nor Ange should in fact have played or be playing the role of Marianne Pearl who is of mixed heritage. The part should have gone to a deserving actress similar to Marianne in terms of looks and heritage within the very small pool of actresses in this category to pick from in Hollywood.

I know it is said that you sometimes have to be selfish to be successful, because it brings up the question: Did 'Plan B' buy the rights to bring the attention of the World to such a poignant story or purely as a means of pursuing an Oscar for whomever Brad happened to be involved with at the time of filming? If it was purely in pursuit of the former then the obvious choice for the portrayal of Marianne

Pearl is Eva Mendes being that she shares the same Cuban ancestry with Marianne who is a mixture of Dutch and Cuban. In Eva's absence, that other Eva or a Halle Berry or a Jessica Alba or a Salma Hayek, or a Jennifer Beals or even a Nicole Ari Parker would have equally done justice to the role. It must be said that Marianne herself actually bears some resemblance to Halle Berry (facial bone structure) in some of the pictures of her that I have seen.

By opting for Angelina Jolie, one is tempted to think that this might be yet another form of racial discrimination or minority oppression. A vivid reminder of where the power lies in Hollywood. On the one hand Brangelina appears to be on the side of the downtrodden, but when it matters most, they may not be averse to taking their jobs and livelihoods away from them to enhance their own Careers and personal fortunes. At the end of the day you may be forced to ask: who is fooling whom?

No one except Brad, Jen and Marianne know for sure what the truth is about the stories, however I know as a fellow human being that if most of it were true and I was Jennifer it would indeed leave a bitter taste in the mouth.

Is it me, or do you all think that Ms. Jolie just seems to be the beneficiary of excessive largesse of late; a devoted Brad Pitt, three healthy kids, yet to be released movies, voice overs, pending movie projects, lucrative commercials in Asia, countless number of awards paying homage to her looks in particular etc the list seems endless, she is definitely living proof that doing good deeds has it rewards and it is not always in heaven. In fairness to her she does give a lot in return and even if we all question different aspects of her life, there seems to be very little doubt about her sincerity and commitment when it involves children and charitable ventures.

Spare a thought for Jennifer Aniston though, who must be wondering what happened to the Brad Pitt she knew for seven years, where did he disappear to?

If indeed she is wondering about the brand new Brad, she, apparently is not alone because a telephone poll of 1004 adults conducted by IPSO in conjunction with AOL between December 19-21 2006 indicates that only 2% of those polled picked Brad Pitt as the best celebrity role model in a poll topped by Oprah. Ange was one of only two people to appear on both the best and worst list of role models in the same poll, the other person being Tom Cruise.

America is very big on therapy and I suppose it works for some people. Who knows if Jen would have needed therapy after such a life-changing crisis? Whatever the case, it seems Jen would have also needed to call up on personal strength and support of loved ones in excessive doses as events unfolded.

The reason is not far fetched, without any sugar coats or anything of such in describing what happened, her husband pretty much dumped her for someone she cannot escape from no matter how much she tries.

Even if she were to succeed in avoiding reading or watching Brad and Ange settling into domestic bliss and embarking on international goodwill ventures together, which is almost impossible, there are people on this Earth who have made it their mission in life to remind her, at every opportunity that presents itself. There will always be that person to ask the surprising and maybe not unexpected questions on the past.

Even if she avoids watching the 'E' Network, what about those Magazine covers every single week. Its little wonder that there were reports that the poor woman was seriously considering leaving the United States for good. Imagine that! Unfortunately, in her case a relocation to Mars might still not help her succeed in avoiding the unavoidable.

7

Love Triangle – A Fait Accompli

$\mathcal{S}$ome relationships are borne out of circumstance whilst others are borne as a result of selfishness. The Brad and Ange relationship was borne out of both.

I thought of naming the book 'Love Triangle Made in Heaven' but I realized that this was bound to create a lot more controversy than was necessary, hence the decision to give it a different title. However we cannot escape the fact that fate played a major part in the birth of Brangelina. We all remember that if a certain ravishing lady named Nicole Kidman (first choice), or Catherine Zeta Jones (second choice) both not turned down the chance to be Mrs Smith then Brangelina would not exist and Jen and Brad would still be married for another couple of years at the very least, or forever.

Yes it is true that not all parties are probably ecstatic at the moment and yes not all parties have discovered a 'profound love' such as is felt for tiny tots but as wonderful as things appear for the Jolie-Pitts, are things really that bad for the jilted ex wife. People tend to think divorce is really horrible, I am not advocating it by any means, but once one or both parties give up on the relationship for whatever reason (usually adultery or lust for a 3rd party), you find in such cases that they suddenly develop a resentment towards their spouse and cannot get out of the Marriage fast enough, divorce may therefore be the best solution in such circumstances.

I realize it is stating the obvious to say that if only that scoundrel that should never have been let out of his vivarium known also as Scott Peterson had had the decency and courage to seek a divorce from his wife Laci, she and Connor would be alive and well today. It is worth mentioning because there are so many cases where spouses or exes harm or kill one another sometimes along with children that I cannot help but think Jennifer must have thanked her lucky stars after all the dust settled on the divorce papers.

Another fact that must be a source of relief to Jennifer is that which plagued her during and after the Marriage, no kids involved. How thankful must Jen be now that she never had kids with Brad, imagine her listening to the kids gushing about Ange after a weekend with Brad. That may have been the straw that finally broke the camel's back.

Maybe the high profile nature of cases like that of Scott Peterson and that of O.J. Simpson are now helping to deter would be murderers of spouses, whatever the case, we are glad that Jen is still here with us and doing very well too. I am by no means suggesting that there was a remote chance of a crime of that nature being committed by any of the parties in this case given the notoriety of the parties, what was at stake and what was likely to be lost, it would have been almost incomprehensible for such a plot to be hatched or contemplated in the circumstances. The lesson here is that divorce as bad as it may be at the time is always a better option than murder.

There has been a lot said by different people in

all aspects of life about the key people in this love triangle but anyone will agree that the most careless remark made so far was made by actress Rosario Dawson on the MTV Program, TRL not too long ago whilst talking about her upcoming movie Sin City 2, whose director reportedly wanted Angelina for a major part in the movie.

Most Careless Remark So Far

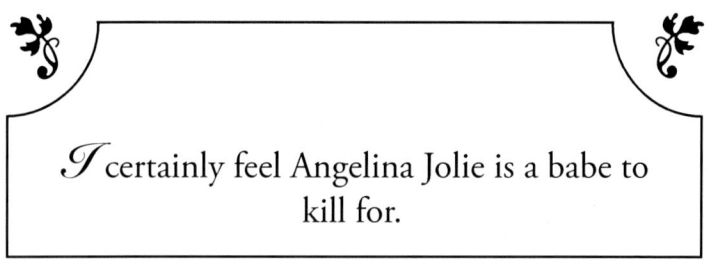

I certainly feel Angelina Jolie is a babe to kill for.

Maybe I am still kind of naïve, but I am always disappointed when I think certain people should talk and act responsibly at all times and they choose not to. One must not forget that MTV programs are targeted at the young adult generation.

8

What If I Were Angelina Jolie?

One of the key questions that come to mind is: If one was in Ange's shoes what would one do or what would one have done? The answer might not be as straightforward as all that. Imagine you were Ange, twice divorced single mother, her last husband walked out on her, although she was finding fulfillment on the humanitarian front, her Career was in a lull of sorts due to a number of box office flops one after the other, the most recent of which was Alexander. There was no relationship worth gushing to Mom about; it was looking as if really decent men were an endangered species.

Enter Mr. Bradley William Pitt, Hollywood heavyweight, nearly top of the enviable A list, one of select individuals twice voted Sexiest Man Alive, worth 100 million dollars and counting, totally smitten, ready to give up anyone and anything for her and ready to give her everything that was missing from her life, a 'troy knight' in shining Armour, what was she supposed to do? I mean Seriously! Yes you can argue that in the circumstances she should have felt some sympathy for Jen and sent Brad back to his wife.

Even outside the Hollywood set up it would have been rare for the ordinary woman to give all that up not to mention the Show Business World where the words 'loyalty', 'trustworthy', 'faithful', 'dependable', 'in sickness and in health' and 'till death us do part' all have a completely different meaning from the normal meaning. In addition to all the above considerations, another fact which might have been key was that Ange was not really acquainted with or friends with Jennifer in the strictest sense. They barely knew each other.

Ange herself said it best long time ago (as if she

knew her tactics then would always be useful) when discussing her Oscar winning performance in 'Girl Interrupted' that she quite deliberately did not want to be close to Winona Rider on the set because she, Ange, could not interact with her and discover that she maybe had a headache in the morning and still attack her as the role required. She needed not to be sensitive to Winona just as she was clearly insensitive to Jennifer.

This is quite different from a Denise Richards and Heather Locklear situation, which was a clear case of betrayal of trust and of a close "friendship". I am tempted to speak directly to Mr. Sambora, which is of course almost impossible. But if it were possible, I would ask him if he felt it necessary to pay back his wife in the manner he has chosen. Or could he have been eyeing callous Richards all along. After two quick kids in succession with her ex (whom she now absolutely despises), don't ask me why but am guessing she had two consecutive C Sections or else (who knows, love may indeed be blind or at the very least blindfolded in Mr. Sambora's case). Sorry little Ms. "he was just too good to pass on" Richards, am only saying or in this case writing what a lot of other people are also thinking about the whole sordid affair.

Granted, the manner Heather went about the whole divorce issue was rather "shambolic" (whatever that means) to say the least. Ms. Heather should have had a lengthy telecon with Dr. Phil before filing those papers. He would have reminded her that you do not throw ten relatively peaceful years of Marriage that produced a beautiful child down the drain in the manner in which she did. The poor guy reportedly found out about the divorce on the radio for chrissakes. There is no excuse for that at all. Even Angelina Jolie might never be able to top that for lack of good taste.

Finally, Mr. Sambora, I would be very wary of knocking up your gal pal anytime soon if I were you, or are you the only one left on the planet that does not know that it seems to bring out the worst in her. Alternatively, you can just put some additional funds aside for your attorneys, you may be needing their additional services even sooner than you imagined.

On a personal note, I have expanded my daily prayers to include the following prayer, because of the likes of Denise Richards that are scattered all over the world:

Prayer

Lord I pray that no member of my immediate family ever become friends or acquaintances with or be compromised in any manner by a Judas type individual like Denise Richards in our lifetimes, Amen.

This is an important prayer because in life you just never know who can turn against you at any moment, so you better pray to God to keep such people far away from you and your loved ones in advance.

Back to Ms. Jolie, she was clearly faced with a 'dilemma' of sorts although some might argue that it was one that was of her own making. It is possible that the combined spirits of all those angelic souls she has touched in the past couple of years unanimously decided to repay her with a bounty of rewards that included Mr. Pitt. Were he single, it would have made for an almost perfect scenario, but in reality since Mr. Pitt was married at the time, one must ask whether angelic souls would wish so much pain and despair on another soul just to make Ange happy, most probably not.

Poor Jen, (I have been told she really despises

being referred to in this manner, but nothing else depicts the situation in which she found herself at the height of all the speculation, better than those words), her Marriage to Brad did not stand a chance, once Brad began to give Ange the green light making it easier for her to flirt with him and vice versa. They became comfortable in each other's company and certainly became very close very fast on the set, from all accounts.

Although one can apportion some blame to Ange, the fact still remains that she was not married at the time; she did not even appear to be in any serious relationship. Brad on the other hand is the one that really needs to examine his conscience because when you get married (whether in Hollywood or outside Hollywood), that union, that ceremony and all that went into it should account for a lot of responsibility, respectability and honor.

It should be the driving force in the lives of the partakers, determining their values, their relationships and interactions with other people whose actions are likely to impact on the Marriage in whatever form.

Of course I am not considering the very popular and usually ill-conceived Las Vegas quickies to be valid members of the institution of Marriage by any stretch of the imagination

Marriage is supposed to be for better or worse and forever. Marriage should not be treated merely as the next step in a relationship. As for Brad, he was in his late thirties when he married Jen, he was not 18 or 20. This was an age where Marriage and all it entails should have been clear to him, especially the responsibility that comes with it.

As far as we know, he was lucid at the time of the Marriage and it was definitely no short gun affair by any means. He it was that should have kept his distance from Ange for the sake of his Marriage, but he chose not to, in the face of the first valid test of the vows of Marriage (that of forsaking all others), Brad Pitt failed miserably. We all hope for his sake that he never lives to regret his actions on that set.

For Jen, that bittersweet quote in the famous first interview post separation from Brad, about always loving him till the end of time may still come back to haunt her in her new relationship(s), especially considering the speed with which Brad moved on and settled into his new role as Mr. Jolie. All of a sudden we see Brad here, there and everywhere with ready made family in tow, helping the United Nations, donating to Orphanages in Africa, undertaking relief work in Pakistan and Haiti, the hair color changed a couple of times and he began looking more and more like Ange as the days went by.

One almost had to do a double take and ask for Brad Pitt to be returned to us from where ever he was hiding. As I mentioned before one must assume that Jen must have been as shocked and astonished as the rest of the world at this "sudden transformation".

It seemed to an onlooker such as myself that Brad pretended to Jennifer till the very end, throwing her a lavish birthday party, denying any romantic links to Ange whatsoever and promising her that they will always be friends and all that. The pretence was very necessary to aid him in fast tracking the divorce and getting what he wanted most out of the Marriage, Plan B Productions, without a hitch and it worked like magic, guess Brad is not as dumb as his looks sometimes suggests, after all.

Burning Question

She must have asked herself the questions we were all asking each other i.e. if you wanted kids so badly and so soon and was so eager to save the World why could we not do all these things together?

I am guessing Brad's answer to that question if he had ever been asked, may have been something like this: Sorry Jen there is only one Angelina Jolie. She is my hero and I want to do all these things with her and no one else, I only put you through that charade of a Marriage we had together because she was not available at the time we got hitched. Ouch.

9

What if Angelina Jolie Were of Color?

*I*t occurred to me at some point whilst writing this book that something a lot of people would not have thought of is that to do with that most sensitive of topics, color and race. I mean, what if our very dear Angelina Jolie was black or to put it more delicately 'not white'? Would Brad still be so smitten? Would he have been smitten at all? Would he have dared leave Jen for her? Would she even have been offered the role of Mrs. Smith to start with? Unfortunately although this is the year 2006, but these are issues that are still so relevant today. Look at what is happening to Madonna because she adopted a black child. She said in an interview that people are stopping her on the streets to ask her why she would adopt such a child. What does this say about society today that has not been said before?

The perfect example of what is wrong with the powers that be and how misguided they are if one is trying to avoid the subject of politics and politicians is that famous Janet Jackson Superbowl exposure debacle. The whole World remembers what Justin Timberlake and Janet Jackson did that resulted in her left or right breast particularly her left or right nipple being exposed during a performance at half time. That incident is not that news worthy, what is news worthy is what transpired afterwards, the craziness that took over which led to a huge outcry, massive uproars, finger pointing, fines and suspensions, intervention of Congress and huge losses of income for Ms. Jackson especially.

In the wake of all that, Justin Timberlake distanced himself immediately from Janet and would not even attend a function that she was also going to be at. The Networks that would have nothing to do with Janet all embraced Justin. Whilst she became an overnight pariah, he was celebrated by all and sundry. This was all rather amazing considering that he was the one that facilitated the act of exposure in the first place. Justin proved himself to be as fair weather as they come, how much worse a person or friend is a certain Kevin Federline when compared to Justin in those circumstances is debatable at best.

Its been a couple of years and Janet is still suffering the consequences, her latest album is not receiving any airplay and is selling woefully, God knows how many positions in various organizations her boyfriend Jermaine Dupri has had to vacate in protest at the treatment being meted out to her (what a stand up guy). Justin on the other hand is selling albums as if they are going out of fashion, he has been credited with 'bringing sexy back', he is hosting Award shows all over the place, and his popularity has never been higher. WHAT A TRAVESTY!

Sadly, this is the state of the World today, nowhere more so than in the United States. Can anyone forget the aftermath of Hurricane Katrina? Fortunately for Justin he is now experiencing feelings of remorse or an attack of guilt. Whatever it is, he is now speaking out publicly about the whole thing (some may question the timing of this attack of conscience though i.e. at a time he is flogging a new album). At a recent interview where the whole superbowl incident came up again, he told MTV's John Morris something to the effect that **he did not quite understand the reaction particularly to Janet after the incident except that he has come to realize that this Country is very unforgiving of women in general and is particularly harsh on "ethnic" people.**

That is as succinct as can be in describing the whole episode and to think that eventually came from Justin (the beneficiary of all the good fortune) himself, what more can one say.

As for Justin's relationship with Ms. Diaz, you sort of knew all along that once JT as he is fondly called had another hit record that she would be gone and that has indeed come to pass. Don't ask me why, he just strikes me as that type of guy.

In all fairness to JT however, a poll of ordinary lads indicated some support for JT by agreeing that if one's girlfriend was a striking looking blonde at the beginning of the relationship and then suddenly becomes a scary looking raven haired creature for no apparent reason, they would dump her in a hurry too. On the flipside, one wonders whether all these 'hot' young starlets such as Jessica Biel now queueing up to spend quality time with Mr. Timberlake would ever have given him the time of day had someone like Cameron not given her stamp of approval for a long time by Hollywood standards (about four years).

You may ask what has Janet's breast or Katrina and all the ugly things that followed have to do with Ange. From my own vantage point, not a whole lot except to press home the point that some things happen that are beyond one's control as a human being whilst others happen because we as human beings have the free will to make them happen or not happen.

With regard to Brad and Ange and the birth of Brangelina and all that transpired on the set of Mr. and Mrs. Smith, it is my humble submission that there would be no Brad and Ange, no Brangelina today were Ange black or as I like to put it 'of color'. There are several reasons that have led me to this conclusion.

First you look at Brad's relationship history since he arrived in Hollywood. It is true that he dated a black actress at some point, Mike Tyson's ex wife, Robin Givens. However, that was a very long time ago when he was still a struggling actor. Since he became more successful, there has been no hint of an inter racial relationship of any kind on his part, very similar to his best pal George Clooney who also had a steady relationship with a black actress when he was a nobody and has since not been linked to one since he became an A lister or a Hollywood heavyweight.

Would Ange have been cast opposite Brad if she were black, almost certainly not? This is still a big issue especially as it relates to blockbuster movies. The Studios want to make a profit and by casting a black actress as Mrs. Smith they most certainly may have recorded huge losses. Even a mega star like Will Smith in a romantic role like the one he portrayed in Hitch confessed that the casting of his love interest in the movie took a lot of deliberation before they agreed on Eva Mendes to sort of make everyone happy. Blacks would not boycott the movie in protest of him falling in love with a white woman and whites would not be offended by that scenario either since Eva is not white perse. A black female lead would have turned the movie into a black movie, which normally translates into poor box office returns, (like 'The Fighting Temptations' with Beyonce Knowles and Cuba Gooding Jr.).

In keeping with tradition, the much acclaimed 'Dreamgirls' movie (musical) was snubbed in the highly coveted best picture category at the Academy Awards, announced as I was proof reading this book prompting me to insert this paragraph to my amendments to the proof. This is the first time in the history of the Oscars that a movie with eight nominations will be so snubbed but as it is a black movie, lets just say the snob did not make the earth shatter into tiny fragments. It was definitely not as shocking to some as it may have been to a few others.

Ironically, the issue of Ange not being of color is now dogging her in her controversial new movie role where she plays the part of Marianne Pearl.

Would Brad have left Jen for a black or ethnic Ange? In my opinion, most certainly not. With all the risk associated with her in terms of her sexuality, love life and all that, the color thing may have been one gamble too many even for Brad (possession of certain Mother Theresa qualities or not).

What all these means is that although we often are not in control of whom we happen to fall in love with, there are times when we can control that emotion or hold it in check so much that it does not alter our lives when we do not want it to do so.

It is by no means a reciprocal thing with regard to the opposite side of the spectrum. In fact the reverse is the case for people of color, unfortunately. This is because a lot of very successful black people particularly athletes end up with white partners for reasons best known to themselves.

A good example is Tiger Woods (who of course prefers not to be labeled black by any stretch of the imagination). After watching him being interviewed a number of times by various people a couple of years back, it was abundantly clear to anyone over ten years old that he would never have married a person of color. Some years later, as expected, when the time came for Tiger to say I do, he went to the land of Volvo whose second biggest export 'commodity' are authentic blonde bombshells (not the bottle type) and selected one for himself.

Black girls (they are usually so young) are only good to be their baby mama's and not much else as propagated by the Gangsta lyrics and Gangsta ("50 Cent") lifestyle that is so common all over the place nowadays. Sean Combs (Bad boy, P. Diddy, Diddy, Diddly, Diddle doo, Doodley or whatever he now prefers to call himself), is a perfect example of this sad culture. His widely reported general irresponsible behaviour barely weeks after his long term girlfriend gave birth to his twins sums up the whole situation nicely indeed. Thank God men like

Lupe Fiasco with his positive lyrics still exist in that Gangsta World however. Obviously the baby mama's themselves cannot be absolved from blame entirely because there is more to life than bling, but they do not seem to know any better. They always seem to choose the harder path to follow and in the process they bring innocent little ones into the World when they are least prepared for them. A lot of black children in America are growing up today without Father figures and with Mothers that have absolutely no idea what they are doing.

Who or what is to blame for so many people's warped perspective on life in general? Can blame be apportioned fairly in the circumstances? As with so many issues raised in this book, the issue of racial prejudice is very much still up in the air.

10

The Media Frenzy

The fascination with the three people in this triangle is unbelievable. Really, how many Magazine covers have they sold between them. You have to ask why wont this story go away, after all couples divorce all the time and no where more so than in Hollywood. In the case of Jennifer Aniston, Brad Pitt and Angelina Jolie however, the reasons are not far fetched, we look at them and we see movie stars the way they are supposed to look, smoking hot, beautiful, sexy, perfect bodies, fullest lips, longest legs, great abs and the list just goes on and on and on and we can't get enough.

Another reason is that those everyday desertions or separations or divorces are rather mundane when compared to this one, the everyday type is not branded and is not chronicled in all available media outlets on the planet. Especially if one remembers that this could almost be said to have been coutured by the media, remember all the alarm bells that went off when it was confirmed that a certain Ange will be starring opposite Brad Pitt in Mr. and Mrs. Smith. The one I remember most clearly read: "Should Jennifer be Worried". With the benefit of hindsight, we now know that everyone was quite right to be worried, none more so than the lady fondly named 'America's Sweetheart'.

In the case of Brad, Ange and Jen however, we all know practically everything (as much as is humanly possible to know), without even trying, about these three whom we are not likely to ever meet or interact with in our lifetimes. All it merely took was for you to be alive, you did not even have to do much except maybe keep your eyes open in supermarket checkout points and the tabloid headlines will beckon to you, or just leave your television set on for any length of time, and you will be finding out a few more things about our subjects that you did not already know.

Yes they seem to always be on Magazine covers, on our small screens and even when we venture out to the cinema they are there waiting for us. Most of all, we must never lose track of what we are never allowed to forget about them, the lips, the bodies, the sexiness, the beauty, and in some cases the hair, etc, etc, but lest one forgets what should really be important, there actually also exists the combined depth of talent.

This is a story that just won't go away, how can it. People usually find excess in others appealing or interesting. This is a story of abundance, abundance of looks, abundance of wealth and abundance of intrigue. Yes, fascination comes with the territory. Even when they protest and lament the extent of intrusion, we cannot bring ourselves to feel sorry for them because we always remember they went out of their way to court the media and sometimes manipulate this medium to their own advantage for any number of reasons in the past.

Ms. Joan Rivers on Larry King Live made the funniest remark in my humble opinion regarding the split. There was still a lot of speculation at the time as to why Brad and Jen were going their separate ways and Larry asked Joan what her thoughts were on it and she gave the following response.

Funniest Quote

Who knows why they are separating, frankly, I think its because she finally saw him in "Troy".

It seems to me that in the case of the Jolie-Pitts (Brangelina) in particular, there is a bandwagon mentality or movement taking over the world. Almost all entertainment and lifestyle organizations cannot wait to be card-carrying members of the caboodle. It has reached ridiculously dizzying heights. I guess the Jolie-Pitts can always send a thank you card to the original Bennifer whenever they become overwhelmed with gratitude for all the 'unwanted' attention.

These are the same group of individuals, those paparazzi, that are now giving us all the impression that it is better for a one year old child to die from malaria or pneumonia than be adopted by Madonna. Where were all these people when Angelina adopted an Ethiopian child? What makes her a better candidate to be an adoptive Parent than Madonna? It has been reported that there are as much as a million orphans in the tiny nation of Malawi alone.

These sorry individuals in the press will never adopt a child in their lifetimes and they are now doing their best to prevent people that genuinely wish to help these suffering children from doing so. How cruel is that?

Its gotten to a point where the paparazzi or should I say the Brangelina fan club, will credit their idols with anything and everything possible. We all know that Nicole Kidman and Tom Cruise adopted two children at least six years before Angelina or Brangelina ever did. Their son Connor is black and from all indications the two children are doing great. I will not however be too surprised at this point to hear that Nicole decided to adopt those children after having lunch with Angelina. We never heard so much praise heaped on Nicole for adopting when she did. The fan club will probably explain the reason for this by saying there is a difference between an adoption that seemed to be borne out of necessity and one that was done on humane grounds. Who knows what they will say, its just plain ridiculous to elevate someone to Mother Theresa status to fill a void and then try to discredit everyone else who are also doing good things for children or people in general.

You will recall that Nicole had to issue various statements recently denying press reports that she passed disparaging remarks about 'Holy Angelina' in relation to her United Nations work. Why should Nicole need to address this sort of garbage, merely because she is also now doing very useful work for the UN? Nicole says her Mom pointed her in the direction of the UN, the paparazzi sorry fan club say Angelina did. Have a heart people. I shudder to imagine what will be written about a certain Jennifer should she ever decide to take up any UN projects, scary.

Still on the craze for Brangelina, imagine a human being posing as a Federal Agent with fake documents and a fake government car just so he can be put on the Brangelina security detail. This sorry excuse for a person is now in custody with no bail and may end up in prison for at least three years, double wow. Lest I forget, what about Mr. Clint Brewer (another dignified member of the paparazzi) that scaled the fence of little Maddox' Day Care or Pre School for pictures of the five year old. Yes, only in Hollywood for damn sure.

Is there any point in mentioning the lengths the paparazzi have gone merely to snap pictures of the loved up family doing ordinary everyday stuff. Can you imagine the poor folks having to escape to Namibia to give birth, un "bleep" believable. I have never been a fan of swearing and am not about to change now, not even for Brangelina, thank you.

If anyone needs any reminder of how crazy it has become, just look at what went on with them in India, whilst filming the Danny Pearl movie.

The usually dependable CNN even had a special programme on the antics of the paparazzi recently, which was aptly titled **"Chasing Angelina"**. I mean, we are still digesting the news that pictures of a baby that was barely four weeks old at the time, sold for an amount in the region of five million dollars (that is UNITED STATES DOLLARS to avoid any confusion on currency and value) I will not even begin to attempt to convert that amount into some currencies of some Third World Countries, a number of people might discover they are suffering from epileptic fits they never knew about until now, better not.

But it gets more interesting by the day because we are now hearing that eight weeks old (as of July 2006), Shiloh Nouvel Jolie-Pitt has also received a one of a kind tribute at the famed Wax Museum, Madame Tussauds in New York, her very own wax figure complete with all the trimmings. Surprise, surprise, she has been placed in front of the wax figures of her Parents.

The fall out of this most questionable action (c'mon we are talking of an eight week old baby) undertaken by the famous Wax Museum which has tied a charity angle to the whole thing is the insensitivity angle as well, sensitivity being a 'chip' or 'gene' we all know a certain Bradley missed out on in the midst of being blessed with so many other wonderful genes. The reason is simple, the Jolie-Pitts have three children, and this is a well-known fact that they never forget to remind us of. Why then would Madame Tussauds choose to put the wax figure of only baby Shiloh with those of Brad and Ange, what happened to the wax figures of Maddox and Zahara?

How will these two feel when they grow up and are able to understand subtle undertones and interpretations of the actions of adults who are supposed to know better? It is possible that the word adoption may come up in any explanation given by the Museum, that is if they even bother to explain. Already you can begin to tell that some issues that may ultimately impact negatively on the relationship of the Jolie-Pitts in future particularly with regard to their offspring may not even be of their own making, but created instead by outside forces beyond their control. Although some might argue that if you sell your baby's pictures then you should expect whatever reactions you get as a result.

Still on the subject of baby Shiloh, at her age it is usually difficult to tell if a child is a boy or a girl merely from looking at the pictures. One way to tell is from the colors that they are dressed by their Parents, usually by Mummy. However, in the pictures released to the World, Shiloh was dressed in blue and white which are normally associated with little boys. I am not trying to read much into this except that it made me wonder if there was any truth to the whisperings that Mama Jolie has indicated that she will not be dressing up her baby in any girlie colors especially pink anytime soon and she allegedly made good on this resolve by not using any of the pink stuff that was gifted her by Brad's Parents.

If this is true, (as reported in the Sun, U.K.), what a tough mama that lady is gonna be, I mean ignoring gifts from Grandparents for such a frivolous reason seems more dis- courteous than resolute in my opinion, it shows a lack of respect on the part of whoever chooses to behave this way, especially where elderly people's feelings are involved. Maybe someone needs to let her know that dressing a girl in pink does not increase her chances of growing up to be "pink" on MTV, although its possible to imagine that the thought alone might be scary enough for most Parents. Having said all that, I must acknowledge that she does have a right to dress up her kids the way she wants, of course, at least until the revolt commences. The revolt will surely come, nowadays its much earlier, say from about eight years old, what's momma gonna do then, we shall see.

On the Ethiopian born Zahara, one is happy to note that the concerns that she may grow up confused and de cultured as a result of being raised exclusively by white Parents can easily be laid to rest by her Parents. They can do so by convincing their superstar, mega rich pals to also adopt African children.

Since Madonna categorically states that they had nothing to do with her decision to adopt an African child, we will be waiting eagerly to see who is next amongst the likes of TomKat, Gwen Stefani, George Clooney, Matt Damon, Wyclef Jean, Julia Roberts, Jamie Oliver and Don Cheadle amongst others, to feel the adoption urge. It seems that the chronic bachelors amongst them might find it a bit harder to file adoption papers though, they may however decide to follow the Leonardo di Caprio option of supporting an Orphanage because of a specific child which might not impact directly on Zahara but is still very useful to society. Having said all that, I will not be holding my breath for George Clooney to follow any such lead anytime soon for obvious reasons..

Contrary to what we all assumed, Zahara should therefore have enough colored friends around her to maybe go to school with and grow up with (sort of like those famous for nothing friends, Paris and Nicole), enough to help her adjust to her new life.

As far as the media frenzy goes, below is a list of titles accorded the Jolie-Pitts in recent months by various media outlets:

1. World's Most Beautiful Family;
2. World's Most Beautiful Woman;
3. World's Sexiest Mom;
4. World's Sexiest Dad;
5. Hollywood's Hottest Mom;
6. Hollywood's Hottest Dad;
7. Maddox Jolie-Pitt- Hollywood's best looking celebrity tot;
8. Summers No.1 Hottest Dad-Brad Pitt;
9. Summers No.1 Hottest Mom-Angelina Jolie;
10. Hollywood's Best Looking Couple
11. Hollywood's Best Looking Parents

Add to these, various comments from people on

those Entertainment Networks always alluding to the fact that they are the Sexiest Couple ever in the history of Film and Cinema or the Couple with the best combined genes and body parts on the planet and you begin to get the general picture.

The list of accolades generally worshipping Brangelina's looks and bodies are endless. Needless to say, about 75% of these accolades are from the 'E' Entertainment Channel or E Network. Yes, that Network that thrives on quality programming such as **'Taradise', 'Girls of the Playboy Mansion', 'Naked Wild On', 'Sexiest', 'House of Carters' and 'Dr. 90210'.** The Network that seems to exist to glorify Brangelina. The same Network that was established after someone had a wet dream about Ms. Jolie. If you need any proof of how shallow human beings are I refer you to their Daily Ten (D10) entertainment news program aired on weekdays.

You only need to watch this once and you will be forced to come to the conclusion that some of the producers and presenters of that show either grew up in Vain County USA or they are hoping to do some kind of business with Brangelina at some point in their lives.

It would appear that their combined brains have long since been fried by all the chemicals they must be exposed to on a daily basis around Hollywood which makes it difficult for them to see beyond their own shallowness, a point which a popular new show like Ugly Betty drives home to everyone else. Especially Ms. Debbie yes I am glad I was fired from "The View" proud to be Greek Matenopoulos. Have you ever seen a worse case of ass licking in your life, whenever she talks about Ange or Brad?

This is the same character that said recently on that same show that it would have been a travesty for Ange and Brad not to have hooked up because they look so good together. Does she know the meaning of the word, I doubt it very much. I will be truly amazed to discover that she doesn't show up for "work" everyday in a 'Team Jolie' T. Shirt.

Just when I was beginning to think I may have been a bit too hard on her, I heard her say that Cameron Diaz looked fantastic and stunning in the ridiculous dress she wore to the Golden Globes (January '07) and it finally dawned on me that Ms. Debbie really did not have any clue at all.

This is the same unit of people that picked Martha Stewart as the No.1 on the all time list of bad women in show business ahead of the likes of Anna Nicole and Winona Ryder and of course the darling of the Network, Angelina Jolie did not even make the list. They then decided to label Donald Trump a "chump" for daring to criticize their beloved Angelina on Larry King live for her ill treatment of her Father, failing to recognize the truth about Ange even when it slaps them on the face.

The D10 characters unilaterally credited Brangelina not too long ago with influencing and guiding Madonna on her adoption of little David from Malawi even going as far as to say that Brangelina had schooled her and Guy on the procedure for an African adoption. However when Madonna appeared on Oprah and categorically stated that she had never discussed adoption with Brangelina, that she had in fact never met Angelina Jolie, you would think they would admit their error. Of course not, they chose to carry the story of Madonna's appearance on Oprah whilst carefully leaving out any mention of what she said about their beloved Brangelina and their non-involvement in the adoption of David.

Talk about haphazard reporting at its highest form. The D10 characters have shown clearly that they are ready to be economical with the truth or even engage in a deliberate mis-representation of facts in order to portray Brangelina positively at all cost. SHAME.

These are the same individuals who were

obsessing about the whereabouts of Tom Cruise and Katie Holmes' baby Suri and even questioned her very existence implying that Katie put pillows in her tummy for nine months and gave birth to a stone or something at the hospital earlier in the year, until the Vanity Fair spread on Suri and her Parents finally shut them up. Really, what type of human beings are these? One cannot help but wonder!

I suggest this D10 entourage spend more time with the Soupy Mr. Joel Mchale of the same Network to help them lighten up a bit and stop taking themselves so seriously. They might also learn that there is more to life than looks especially the plastic type Hollywood is so well known for.

Needless to say that if only such countless awards and honors bestowed on the couple can be translated into pledges and donations, the sheer quantity would guarantee that there will be more money available to fund charitable organizations helping orphans and refugees in Africa, two causes that are particularly dear to their beloved Brangelina.

On an international level, The E True Hollywood Story 'THS' (on that same Network) has been broadcasting the true life story of Angelina Jolie and others like her that they deemed deserving, about four times a week on the average in Europe and Africa (the latter being the Continent that Ms. Jolie loves so much). What this means is that in one calender year, each programme might air or be repeated, not less than one hundred and ninety two (192) times, wow.

It goes without saying that a lot more students who were fortunate or unfortunate enough (depends), to have been exposed to this telecast will probably score higher marks in a Ms. Jolie quiz than in their math exam for example. I mean who wants to be sitting for a math exam or worse still study for it, except you are come back queen Ms. Teri Hatcher of course, (remember she studied Engineering and Math in College) who says there are no beauty and brain combinations in Hollywood.

Some actresses with these great combo include Oscar winner, Reese Witherspoon, Natalie Portman, Brooke Shields, Lisa Kudrow, Anne Hathaway, Amanda Peet, Jennifer Garner and not forgetting my fellow alumnus, British actress Ms. Thandi Newton who studied at Cambridge. I still look back at that period of my life with great fondness. At the risk of sounding condescending which is certainly not my intention, it is not surprising that the beauty and brain combo are indeed few and far between in Hollywood. This may be for the simple reason that it is or it seems extremely difficult to pursue both or possess both, who knows?

Going back to Ms. Teri Hatcher who also happens to be one of my favorite actresses, thank God she came to her senses very fast on the issue of dating a certain Mr. Ryan "Hugh Hefner is my hero" Seacrest, also of the "um high quality" E Network who looked more like her valet attendant than anything else and should never have been in the picture to start with. As for our favorite ER doctor, George Clooney, it was not too surprising to discover the treatment he meted out to Ms. Hatcher who apparently showed some interest in him and he was rather dismissive, (probably felt she was too old for him, being above 25 years).

It was quite heartwarming to find out recently that Teri has since found true love with someone she describes as perfect. I wish her happiness and peace with a good dose of good luck this time around, she deserves it.

Oh dear have I digressed completely or what, I must have run out of coffee again.

Back to the point, in spite of all the sucking up to Brangelina by the media however, it is worthwhile to still point out that recent polls conducted in the U.S. by some of these same media outlets on the people that matter i.e. the fans, still indicate that America's

Sweetheart is still more popular than the Brad and Ange combo in a lot of quarters. She was voted tops as favorite 'All American' in an Independence day (July 4th) poll conducted by Entertainment Tonight. If I were to hazard a guess I would say that I think that must have left a bitter taste in the mouth of some people especially that mouth which is covered by those most luscious of all lips.

Also, in spite of all the sucking up by the E Network, particularly the D10 individuals, Brad has apparently also had enough because according to People Magazine (you know the ones that told us that Britney Spears' new born's names are Sutton, Pierce when they were in fact Jayden, James), his attorneys have just filed a trespass law suit against that Network and one of its producers for strolling into his Hollywood Hills home without permission with a cameraman in tow whilst ostensibly researching a project on Brad that the Network is working on, probably an E 'THS' type thing, (an 'E' specialty of sorts). If it is indeed true, sorry guys, am guessing you thought you were welcome at your best pals home at any time, at the very least, as payback for all those awards. What a way for Brad to say thank you for all the ass licking and adulation. Good on you Brad. Enough already.

As for Brad being named best Dad this and best Dad that, you almost have to remind yourself that his application to adopt Ange's kids was filed less than a year ago and baby Shiloh is still a baby, yes. As for the adoption application, I think we can safely assume that Brad did not ask Jen for a reference on character in order to comply with some of the mandatory requirements for such a process.

Are we to believe that Hollywood is devoid of Parents who have teenage kids that are in college and doing great in life generally? I guess the older Dad's in Hollywood pale in comparison to huge biceps and six packs. Needless to say, all these accolades heaped on these two may not be endearing them to too many people in their neighborhood.

I am not the only one aware that not all Hollywood kids grow up to be a Paris, Tara or Nicole (Ritchie). Believe it or not, some Hollywood Parents are raising kids that are turning out alright, maybe not necessarily in the Hollywood environment perse.

Do I sense a collective holding of breath until we learn of the demise of the hasty Marriage between a character that left his wife of over a decade and two kids in Canada (one of them very young), for a heiress to a mega fortune named Tori who only just found out that her inheritance in liquid cash is a mere six figure amount, extremely very little by Hollywood standards. Then the painful process (or ritual) of emancipating the body from those hideous tattoos will begin, again. Do they ever learn? No way.

As for me, I am so tired of the Brangelina furore now that were I to be a member of the Oscar Voting Committee (of course this is not remotely possible) and one of the two principal actors or both were to be nominated for an Oscar they will not be getting my vote not because of any animosity towards them but simply because other people also deserve to get what they want in life.

All that joy, happiness and reward for hard work and personal endeavor should be spread out as widely as possible, if only to ensure that they know that they are also ripe for some form of disappointment in whatever form at some point in their lives. I will simply be helping to spread the message that in life you don't always get what you deserve, like all mere mortals experience occasionally or frequently, depending on luck.

It seems a lot more people share my views in Hollywood than they are letting on because the Oscar nominations have just been announced and Brad Pitt's performance in Babel was ignored. Who knows, It could be that the voters found all the sudden praise heaped on his performance by ex fiancee, Gwyneth Paltrow a bit too biased.

On a more sincere note however, you have to say that if Brad did not receive an Oscar for his performances in "Legends of the Fall" (not nominated) and the two others for which he was nominated (in the supporting category), he may have missed his chance to ever win one.

Still on the subject of awards, what are Jen's chances of ever winning an Oscar? I don't think am the only one not holding my breath on that one. You just wonder what she can do to make it happen and you cannot really see it. Not that she is not deserving or good enough but because she has unconsciously been typecast as a pure comic and comedic roles hardly ever win, period. Definitely an actor that can keep a very straight face whilst delivering a line that says "she was on vacation" to a remark about her sister having slept with the entire Arizona Cardinals frontline in the 'Breakup' (and she did it with some degree of seriousness and conviction too), does possess acting chops or doesn't she? Does she even desire one though? If the answer is YES, which I suspect to be the case, it seems this might be one of the other disappointments of her life or should I say career. Fingers crossed on that one.

Above all else, although we all realize that the media does not owe Jennifer Aniston anything, she is a big girl and all that, you cannot help but be compelled to feel sorry for her even when she begs you not too. You feel sorry not because she went through a divorce, not because she fell in love with someone that broke her heart (shattered it into tiny fragments) and certainly not because she deserves it more than the next person, but because the media, that all powerful, all knowing institution have made it their mission in life not to let her forget that her husband dumped her for the world's sexiest this and most attractive, full lipped that. I mean it got to the point where relocating to another Continent, specifically to Australia from the U.S. was apparently looking very appealing to her. Unfortunately, even that might not be far enough.

From all indications relocating to Greece may even be out of the question (remember Jen is of Greek ancestry from Daddy's side of the family). This is because Ms. Jolie is apparently quite popular there too. She has just been named Maxim Magazine Greece's 'Woman of the Year'. If this is not an irony, I don't know what is.

You do not have to be a female to imagine how degrading this never ending comparison is, not to mention what it can do to anyone's self esteem or psyche, especially when the views are always almost parallel. As if that is not enough, poor six pack less Vince also had to suffer the indignity of being polled against Bradley almost on all levels of human existence imaginable. Ouch. Apparently, Brad is also a big fan of his own looks, if we are to believe his best pal George who says that anytime he refers to Brad as 'sexiest male' he happily responds by adding 'twice'.

It is often surprising the lengths human beings sometimes go to be callous or mean to others. People seem to conveniently forget that beauty has always been and will always be in the eyes of the beholder. I look at somebody like Jennifer Aniston and see everything sexy about her that people see in Angelina Jolie without the thick lips, fewer or non existent tattoos except that she definitely needs to wear less black (no more mourning please).

I mean how much black can a person wear without reminding people of funerals. If and when Jen chooses to be seen in livelier more refreshing colors and less matronly designs (I recall the horror she wore to the GQ awards ceremony), then really the World may be exposed to another Jen, a vibrant and trend setting one. Has no one noticed Jen in shorts? The girl has the best legs in Hollywood and I am not exaggerating. Obviously whilst these criticisms of her dress sense may be regarded as shortcomings, I certainly do not believe they were enough to lead to divorce.

On a surprising note, People Magazine's online readers definitely do not agree with my views on Jen's dress sense as they recently voted her the best dressed woman in Hollywood for her 'casual and approachable style' of dressing which they feel is as close to normal as a celebrity can dress. Somehow, you just know that she would never have been No.1 if the Magazine's editors were the ones doing the voting as they had always done every year except this one.

On the premise that God did not create any perfect human being, in Jennifer's case the positives definitely far outweigh the negatives. In all fairness, I would have to say that even Ange has been trying her best to try and make the positives of the present outweigh the negatives of the past and she does deserve some credit for that too.

As for the story that Jen has now become a regular sleepwalker, if this is true, one can blame that partly on the stress from her failed liasons with Brad and Vince. However, secondary responsibility falls squarely on the media especially the E Network that repeatedly informs the whole World over and over in one million different ways that it was a brilliant idea for Brad to leave his wife for "smoking hot, full lipped" Ms. Jolie. if it was me, I would be sleepwalking too, dammit.

On a funny in an intelligent way mode, Ashley Judd when asked recently to respond to being named in one of those Top 100 Magazine polls to do with all that superficial stuff said the following:

Ashley Judd - Most Intelligent Quote

Wouldn't the World be a better place if that Magazine did not exist?

11

Confirmed, Your Spouse or Partner is Gay Or Bi-sexual

We all know that Angelina Jolie is admittedly bi-sexual. This poses another issue for Brad to deal with on a constant basis in the relationship.

To say this is most unusual is an under statement. C'mon, how many couples do you know who are together and it is common knowledge that one or the other is bi-sexual whilst the significant other is heterosexual?

That does not mean that it cannot work out in the absolute sense. In such a relationship, it seems honesty and trust would be two key issues. Whatever the case, it is going to prove to be a huge test of resolve and character at the very least. Especially now that we are hearing that Ange cannot wait to swap some female spit under cover of shooting a movie. I bet her agents are already on the lookout for any yummy lesbian oriented scripts out there to rival 'Brokeback Mountain'.

Unfortunately for the producers of one of my fave shows, the L Word, a diva like her would never agree to appear on their show now that she is such a huge star.

There are a couple of well known bi-sexuals in Hollywood. Two of the better known ones are Anne Heche and Cynthia Nixon. Anne Heche was actor Steve Martin's girlfriend for several years. Then all of a sudden, she began dating Ellen Degeneres in a very high profile relationship. After a couple of years she parted ways with Ellen and is now married to a man. At the time it was said that Ellen was really devastated by the split. Anne seemed to suffer a nervous breakdown and was found wandering around a neighborhood several miles away from her home in a distressed state and muttering about space ships shortly after the split from Ellen.

This gave rise to a lot of speculation. It seems however that the burden of being bi-sexual was what finally got to Anne and pushed her nearly over the edge. I guess she is still as confused today as she was then because she has now split from her husband after five years of marriage.

In the case of Cynthia Nixon, formerly of "Sex and the City", she was with the Father of her kids for well over a decade. All of a sudden she declared that she was in a relationship with a woman. This came as a shock to everyone. It is not clear whether her former partner was just as shocked as everyone else or whether he knew all along.

Nowadays, we are realizing more and more that shocking people seems to come with the territory in such cases. Not surprisingly, the politicians are not spared either. Who can forget the former New Jersey Governor, Jim McGreevey who turned out to be gay and had to resign from that position in the wake of the scandal that broke out. He has since separated from his wife who is apparently still reeling and has settled down with an Australian Businessman as a potential life partner. More recently House of Rep. Member, Mark Foley who was assumed to be heterosexual was found to have been secretly sending sexually suggestive emails to male interns and also had to resign.

The go to publication for coming out now seems to be 'People Magazine' we are now literarily finding out practically on a weekly basis that a male show business personality was in the closet all along and they now feel the sudden need to free themselves. The attack of conscience seems to be presently contagious.

With someone like Angelina Jolie on the other hand, she openly admits an attraction to females but has only had one public affair with another woman that we are aware of thus far. The issue of her bi-sexuality may however still weigh down the relationship as time goes by. Although it is usually said that men are fascinated by lesbians and always look forward to threesomes with two women. You somehow get the feeling that this might not be the case here.

It may be particularly tough on Brad, whether he admits it or not. Reason is that men and women find Angelina equally attractive. You even have several young Hollywood starlets and actresses on the No.1 Show on American television like Ellen Pompeo openly admitting crushes on her. Brad may probably need to keep employing her through his Production Company for the remainder of her Career.

If he does this, he will carefully be choosing cast mates (male and female) to reduce temptation as much as possible. In the alternative, he may steer her Career towards children through the voice over medium, which is safe from undue interaction with other actors. Also, this may be good for Ange whose focus in life right now are the kids.

Nevertheless, it is a daunting task or prospect for anyone, not least of all Brad. This is because even if the trust element in the relationship is very high, the level of precaution and anxiety may be way higher than in a normal relationship. How much precaution can one partner or spouse undertake in a lifetime or even over a period of time?

From all indications, it appears that women who are bi-sexual can stay in a relationship with a man far longer than men who are gay. Gay men always tend to have very little interest in having a sexual relationship with a woman and even in cases of those in the closet, (on the down low); it is usually a matter of time.

You find in such cases that the rate of infidelity is very high amongst such men and in retrospect their wives would have always sensed that something was not right. In relation to the Jolie-Pitts however, it certainly augurs well for the relationship that Brad is not the gay one, at least as far as we all can tell, for now.

This issue of bi-sexuality is another situation where we will all have to wait and see how it eventually impacts on the relationship of the Jolie-Pitts as it continues to develop.

12

Lessons From the Break-Up

I am one of those that believe that a man with a chronic case of cold feet is better and more honorable than one that marries a woman and treats her like dirt or disrespects her or continues to behave as if he is still single after Marriage.

One of the lessons from the break up of Brad and Jen is that you walk away from something if you do not hold it dear enough to your heart. That is what Brad did. Instead of working out issues with Jen, he chose to start all over with someone else.

One of the most important aspects of Marriage is respect for one's spouse. Once respect is lost or was never reposed, the tendency is for the Marriage to head towards failure, because the person disrespected will not accept that treatment forever.

Respect takes various forms, one of which is to stay away from the danger of being unfaithful or the temptation to be unfaithful. Therefore, when the time comes in a Marriage when you feel some attraction to some other person, a good Marriage candidate i.e. Will Smith would do any number of things.

- If you work in the movie industry for example, you stay away from projects involving such a person;

- If you must work with them, you need to maintain that distance that sends the message that you are strictly after a professional relationship; and

- Intimacy should be limited to the barest minimum between you and that person, if at all. Instead of requesting more steamy stuff to be in the script with that person you make sure you do what is necessary, (request for reduced contact if necessary);

Always Send The Right Message

In the movie 'Hitch' the love story between Will Smith and Eva Mendes was beautiful. There was nothing over the top yet it was still very interesting to watch them interact. Eva Mendes is also a very attractive young lady (some may argue just as attractive or even more attractive than Ange) and single, (though in a steady relationship) but Will still went back to Jada and Eva's relationship is still intact.

• A married person should not act on selfish urges (physical or otherwise) no matter how appealing the other person is or how much enjoyment you think you are going to derive from your act of selfishness;

• Once married, you must tell yourself that whatever you see that is so enticing or magnificent in that other person that you are attracted to can be replicated in your own spouse, if only one is willing to make the effort. For example, if your co-star (the one you like so much) has cute kids on the set everyday, and your paternal hormones are suddenly raging out of control. Please go back home and knock up your wife or at the very least communicate how you are feeling to her;

- When a person leaves his or her spouse for someone else, the chances are high that he or she will do the same thing again. For our purpose, anyone will be right to ask – what is to stop Brad in a couple of years from leaving Ange for any of the three young Jessica's currently heating up Hollywood, for example;

- The point being that if you are not able to stay committed you are not going to be committed. Such a person will always move on once they see something they want somewhere else. Instead of creating what they want with the one they are with, they are likely to keep finding excuses to move on to the next person;

- A responsible married man should not deliberately seek familiarity with off spring of the co-star he is attracted to, to the point where the child soon begins to see that person in a paternal light. Something is definitely not right about that.

- The Bible tells us that if a woman prays continuously to God for her husband not to stray and he still does, she cannot blame herself because the decision to stray is ultimately his. He chose to walk in the flesh instead of in the spirit, this is also applicable to a woman who chooses to stray;

Galatians 5:16,17

Walk in the Spirit, and you shall not fulfill the lust of the flesh. For the flesh lusts against the Spirit, and the Spirit against the flesh; and these are contrary to one another, so that you do not do the things that you wish.

- Where one finds that they are no longer happy with their spouse and they are definitely not willing to try to work things out, then divorce is always a better option than murder;

- Where there is a potential for three people to be deeply hurt or unhappy, would it not be better to make two people ecstatic and hurt only one person badly. This is always a tough one to call, depends on how you see the glass, half empty or half full;

- When you are co owners of a business or entity started together when everything was fine, when a divorce petition shows up, make sure you employ professionals that will actually provide you quality service and earn their high fees by ensuring that you get an equitable share of the business as part of the divorce settlement. This is to avoid a situation where certain decisions of your ex regarding the activities of the business come back to haunt you in the future.

For example, in the case of Jen and Brad and their Production Company, Plan B Productions – we all recall how happy Jen was when she spoke of at least seventeen projects in development as at 2004. Well, guess what, she is no longer a part of Plan B and dear Ange (that name again, am afraid so) has been employed by Brad to star in the role Jen herself was reported to be very much interested in.

It was reported that Jen was very much involved in bringing the project to Plan B, but Ange just showed up and got the role on a platter of gold, in addition to Brad of course, ouch.

The lesson here is, if something is dear to you fight for it, do not leave it in the hands of a scheming ex. Also, we are all now discovering how smart and profitable Plan B Productions is fast becoming, producing films like 'Charlie and the Chocolate Factory' with Johnny Depp and more recently 'The Departed' which was directed by Martin Scorsese with an all star cast that included Jack Nicholson, Leonardo Di Caprio, Matt

Damon, Alec Baldwin and Mark Wahlberg.

The question that comes to mind is whether Jen is benefiting from these successes of the company in any way at this time considering that these were most likely projects she helped to develop, if not you have to conclude that she got the raw end of the divorce settlement;

- When your own Parents are reluctant to endorse your new relationship, particularly if your mother finds it very difficult to cut off from your ex, maybe, you need to pause and take a good look at the whole picture or wake up and smell the coffee;

- The biggest beneficiaries of lessons learnt from the break up are clearly Brad and Ange themselves, because they are suddenly both Marriage shy. Getting married seems to have lost its sparkle for both. In fact according to Ange, they will only get married if the children grow up and demand a wedding. Then and only then will they get married. Whilst according to Brad it will only happen when everyone that wishes to marry can marry. What both statements mean is that Marriage is not on the horizon for this couple anytime soon;

- This already appears to be a smart move on the part of the couple of the moment, as it postpones the date when the media starts to countdown the end of their Marriage. In their case only time will tell what the wisest move was or has been, or will be;

• Where there are no kids involved, a divorce usually ends the relationship completely. It also helps the parties to move on faster and easier.

This is because for every Bruce and Demi there are tens of dozens of the Alecs' and Kims'. On the issue of custody and acrimony, at the rate they are going, the battle between Alec Baldwin and Kim Basinger over their daughter will be a case study for law students for generations to come. I only hope they wake up soon and realize the harm being inflicted on their young daughter by their "grown up" actions.

Already Britney Spears and that paedomorph that she married, Kevin Federline (now Fed-Ex) are beginning to show that they may be the biggest supporters of the Alec and Kim method of divorce, no surprise there whatsoever. The surprise was Britney's Parental figures utter disappearance at the time she made the decision to enter into that union in the first place, because she obviously did not get enough counseling from the people that should have mattered.

After failing their daughter once by encouraging her to marry that person, these same people stood quietly by and did nothing to prevent the World from viewing the horror series 'Chaotic' which finally convinced us all that something is definitely not right with those two. Thank God (for the sake of those little children, if nothing else) that Kanye West whispered the words 'Prenup' loudly enough into the ears of Missus Spears and she heeded some good advice, for a change.

By the way, that was a joke Britney, jokes being something you better get used to now more than ever, you set yourself up big time.

Seriously Britney, did it never occur to you or anyone else close to you that having children for Master Federline means you are tied to him for the rest of your life, pre-nup or not. He has a legal right to visitation in addition to a host of other parental privileges over them (until they are adults at the very least). Those innocent souls will be exposed to him and all he stands for, for years to come, all thanks to you for carefully choosing their Father figure. It begs the question, which option is preferable in this circumstance, a 'K-Fed' Father or an absent Father?

Having observed (along with the rest of the World) Britney's general conduct since she filed for divorce, I now feel inclined to apologise profusely to Mr. Federline for being so hard on him, having put up with her for so long. I mean, SERIOUSLY.

After all is said and done, I only have one question for you my dear: Was sex with Justin that bad?

13

Is Brad Really That Bad?

I know people will say that I have been quite judgmental of Brad and Ange in this book, particularly Brad. That certainly was not my intention. I have merely looked at the facts and have also tried to interpret some of the actions of the key people in the wake of the break up.

In the overall scheme of things or shall I say men, would one say Brad dumping Jen for Ange was the worst conduct attributable to men in the show business fraternity. We all know how common it is for Hollywood relationships to break up, but people break up all the time, it is by no means reserved for people in Hollywood, by any stretch of the imagination.

For the purpose of this book, I will focus on Hollywood relationships. I will look at some past actions of certain show business individuals, just to try and put Brad's recent actions into perspective. I will also be trying to make comparisons where possible.

MR TOM CRUISE

First, I'll compare Brad's actions to that of the very well known Mr. Tom Cruise when he filed for divorce from his second wife of nearly ten years, Nicole Kidman. This news also came out of the blue, I mean they seemed so happy and we all assumed they would always be together, just like Brad and Jen.

It was widely reported at the time that Tom's actions completely blindsided Nicole. That the divorce petition was totally unexpected and caused a lot of distress, which ultimately resulted in the miscarriage by Nicole of the first biological child the couple would have had together. At the time there was the usual speculation about what the various reasons for the separation could have been, the word 'Scientology' came up a few times not surprisingly. It was then suggested that Nicole may have had an affair with that man again, Jude Law, her co-star in the movie 'Hours'. She however dispelled this rumor by successfully suing the Tabloids claiming such and winning damages in return. Tom only said publicly that Nicole knows what she did without saying much further.

After almost ten years of Marriage and a three month old pregnancy, short of a heinous crime being committed by Nicole since adultery was ruled out, one would have expected Tom to try and work things out in his Marriage, but in Hollywood, of course not.

Not too long after the announcement, guess who Tom started stepping out with? Yes, you are right, Ms. Penelope "I'm the Spanish Angelina Jolie" Cruz, his co-star in one of the worst movies ever made anywhere, (in my humble opinion) "Vanilla Sky".

Then it was 'Cruise on Cruz' everywhere for about three years or so until the union fizzled out in the hot Sahara sun of Morocco, allegedly in the arms of another Sexiest Man Alive".

Then came 'Dawsons Creek's" Katie Holmes

two decades his junior, a relationship which is now defined by the Oprah couch jumping extravaganza deeply etched in memory. We all heard utterances such as "I have never been so in love", love, love, love, love, love and more love. Personally, I was breastfeeding my little baby girl at the time of the incident and somehow my breast popped out of her mouth in what I can only describe as 'shock'.

After it all sank in, then one began to wonder if this was the same man that was married to the ravishingly beautiful Nicole Kidman for so long. In fact you wondered if he had had a relationship with a woman prior to Ms. Katie.

On a different subject but still on Mr. Cruise, he it was who also had the temerity to criticize a woman suffering from post natal depression on the method she chose to deal with it successfully. Who died and made Mr. Cruise the sole authority on something he can never experience personally. Even if Mr. Cruise were to undergo a sex change today, what are his chances of getting pregnant. There are people on this Earth who will never know how to quit while they are ahead and Mr. Cruise is well ahead of Brad in this category.

He has since apologized and made up with Brooke, but if anyone is out there thinking it has less to do with Brooke and more to do with gaining back some credibility after the Paramount fall out and to win back some of the Zillion female fans he lost of late, they may not be too far off at all. The coincidence is a bit too glaring to overlook.

MR WOODY ALLEN

Secondly, I will compare Brad's actions to that of one Mr.Woody Allen formerly of New York City who now suddenly feels more at home in London. We all remember how Mr. Woody as I prefer to call him was caught with naked pictures of his then wife (Mia Farrow's), adopted daughter, Soon Yi in his possession. Mia had adopted Soon Yi when she was eight years old and raised her with Allen as her Step Father. Is there any part of this scenario that strikes a vaguely familiar cord, I wonder?

How does a Mia Farrow recover from something like that, suddenly discovering that you were married to someone who was obviously hiding some paedophilic tendencies for so long? Then to add insult to injury, after the all ties to Mia Farrow were completely severed, Mr. Woody then proceeded to marry Soon Yi. A potential winner for "Worst Human Conduct In A Marital Union" if ever there was one.

A little piece of advice to Ms. Scarlett Johansson, I know you have said that you wouldn't mind spending the rest of your Career working with Mr. Woody, I suggest you get all your Woody movies out of your system now, certainly before you start having children and you feel the need to bring your little daughter(s) along to the set daily, enough said.

THE BILLY CRUDUP TYPE

I have been giving a lot of thought to whether I should bother wasting everyone's time by discussing the worst breed of man not created by God, the deserters or plain unconscionable type of individual or for lack of a better word, "Scum". I am referring to the Billy Crudup's and Kevin Federline's of this World that leave their long term partners who are pregnant with their child or children, for another woman at the height of the pregnancy. In this case, their partners namely Mary Louise Parker and Shar Jackson were seven months gone or thereabouts and in the third trimester respectively.

If the reports of being caught in fragrante delicto coming out of the U.S. are true relating to Billy Crudup's girlfriend, Ms. Claire Danes which led to the demise of their relationship around Christmas, then the doubting Thomas's out there must agree that Karma does exist after all.

Yes its true, Tom Cruise was a copycat before he became a TomKat. In most cases, these men are so consumed with lust that they do not give a damn that they are jeopardizing the healths of both their partners and unborn children. In Nicole Kidman's case, the child never had the opportunity to arrive in this World because she suffered a mis-carriage that may have been a result of the distress and all the trauma that accompanied her split from that man, what's his name again.

You just know that the Claire Danes and Britney Spears type of woman that hook up with men like these that made no attempt to hide their callousness and lack of loyalty to another human being as well as to their unborn child, can never and should never complain about anything bad they get out of the relationship with such men, as it is usually only a matter of time.

Ms. Spears is already learning that lesson the hard way, whether she knows it's a lesson or not is another matter entirely.

MATT LE BLANC (SPINELESS TYPE)

More frequently, the man leaves after the child is born with some problem or the other. An example is Matt Le Blanc, "Brad Pitt wannabe" (of 'Friends' and 'Joey') who left his wife recently for his co-star on 'Joey'. What is sad about this is that they have a little child together who reportedly suffers from a rare brain disorder (which may cause seizures). Matt therefore qualifies to be labeled a deserter, one who bails out when the going gets tough or who just bails out because he can. The spineless type of guy.

ERIC BENET (TESTOSTERONE TYPE)

There are also men like Eric Benet who end up marrying a beautiful wife (even beyond their dreams) who also happens to be the breadwinner in the family, but they still find a reason or several reasons to label themselves 'sex addicts'. They find every excuse to blame their actions on their D4 gene suggesting that they are not in complete control of their actions. Such men fool around with every willing participant they can find and even take them to their marital homes in their wife's absence. Of course such men always get what's due to them sooner or later, Eric Benet can testify to this after being booted out by Halle Berry.

GEORGE CLOONEY.

We must not forget Brad's 'best buddy' Mr. George Clooney. They share a lot in common most recent of which is an aversion to Marriage. The George Clooney type of man is not interested in settling down with a single partner. Such men change partners as often as they change their underwear and the mere thought of multiplying through having children is found to be repulsive.

For these kind of men, the prodigal lifestyle is just too attractive to give up.

Such men get carried away with all the accolades they receive which are mostly about their looks. They are therefore unable to gift all that beauty to just one individual. Who can blame them for feeling this way, especially since they truly believe that they are doing a service to mankind by spreading so much love through their manhood. Yes, men like this exist everywhere, especially in Hollywood.

You cannot help but sense that Mr. Clooney needs to be a lot older with only Anna Nicole wannabes having his time of day before it finally dawns on him that serial dating with nothing positive to show for it guarantees a lonely old age for rich and poor alike. Fellow middle-aged actor James Woods will attest to this fact after recently finding out the hard way that he really should not be dating twenty year old girls at this time, in his life. According to several media reports, (this had something to do with his 20 year old ex girlfriend's conduct at his brother's funeral). Talk about learning a simple lesson the hard way.

Ms. JULIA ROBERTS

I know Julia Roberts is not a man, but can one forget that in her day she was just as naughty and bad as any man in Hollywood, maybe even more so than our dearest Ange.

Ms. Roberts started dating Kiefer Sutherland on the set of the movie 'Flatliners' whilst he was still married to someone else. He left his wife for Julia and they got engaged. She then dumped him on the eve of their wedding for his best friend (yes, best friend), Jason Patric. Apparently, Kiefer was found guilty of being naughty with a stripper probably at his bachelor party or something like that. I bet Kiefer was thankful to discover that Jason was not the type of guy he wanted as a part of his life in any capacity. Whatever happened to the guy anyway, I mean, could his disappearance from the acting stratosphere have something to do with karma?

She then dated a lot of fellow actors and shocked herself and the rest of the world by marrying Lyle Lovett. Of course they both came to their senses soon after. Just when we thought it had to be Benjamin Bratt, we found out it would be Danny Moder, a cameraman she met on the set of "The Mexican" starring, you guessed it, Brad Pitt. Danny was still married at the time of course, and he too left his wife for Julia. It seems the more married a man is, the more he becomes attractive to the 'pretty woman'. Anyway, she has since rewarded Danny for his courage to go through with the divorce by giving him a set of twins (a boy and a girl).

THE SORRY I WAS CAUGHT TYPE (JUDE LAW/PETER COOK)

Whilst we are on the subject of comparisons, should we not compare Brad to a Jude

Law, Peter Cook type of guy. After all, they are the ones that are always very sorry that they were caught doing bad things but definitely not sorry for what they did. A careful examination of their fake claims of remorse always shows that they are not really sorry for their inability to control their libido and their lack of uprightness and capacity to be loyal or faithful in a relationship premised on trust. They only wish they had not been caught. I cannot imagine how many Nanny applications Sienna Miller may have to turn down in her lifetime, that is if she is stupid enough to re-visit the on again, off again relationship, long term. Of course, they might decide not to have any children; Jude already has three, remember.

HOLLYWOOD MADAM VERSUS HOLLYWOOD MISSUS

No one will dispute the fact that the burden of keeping a Marriage fresh and interesting lies squarely on the woman's shoulders, is this really fair? That is a question for the ages. This is a fact that applies not just in Hollywood but also practically everywhere on the planet.

A man can grow bald, have a potbelly or even lose a couple of balls and its ok. A woman on the other hand must stay paper thin at all times. Nowadays, having babies is no longer an excuse to be fat thanks to supermodel, Heidi Klum who was back on the catwalk looking very trim, a couple of weeks after giving birth, and all those actresses as well, some of whom opt out of breast feeding in favor of getting their figures back in two to four weeks or less.

Its not just the slim figure any longer, you look at a Jennifer for example, and you ask yourself – does she make enough trips to Victoria Secret for sexy lingerie? You may also be tempted to ask whether she stocks up on all the latest toys from places like Agent Provocateur. If you are like me thinking, maybe not, then we must be in the majority.

An Angelina on the other hand strikes you as one that stocks up regularly on all those gadgets, religiously perhaps. She's been known to disclose her fondness for those types of toys. This may ultimately have been what tipped the scales in her favor where Brad was concerned. Especially if one recalls that Brad used to be a stripper pimp, back in the day. Believe it or not, there is a Charlie Sheen in every man. The difference is that some men would prefer to do all those 'nice' things with their wives, some others would prefer to pay for it and there are those that will choose to look elsewhere entirely for it.

For the married man who chooses to pay for it or look elsewhere, in future, I suggest that you try the option of discussing your desires with your wife or even cajoling if necessary. What does it matter how you got it as long as you get what you want. This is a better option to jumping ship altogether or jeopardizing your Marriage by visiting prostitutes, unless of course your Marriage meant very little to you to start with.

THE GOOD GUYS

On the flip side, what about comparing Brad to the great husbands of Hollywood, such as the Paul Newman's, John Travolta's, Will Smith's, Blair Underwood's, William H. Macy's, Kevin Bacon's, Mathew Broderick's and David Arquette's and so on to see how he measures up. If you think he measures up pretty poorly, you may be absolutely right.

For no other reason, other than the fact that these guys understand what Marriage and responsibility are all about. They understand the meaning of sharing ones life with another human being for better or for worse, especially that part about forsaking all others.

WILL SMITH

Take a Will Smith, yes it's his second Marriage, but the first Marriage took place when he was very young. The adolescent Will is a very different man from the one married to Jada Pinkett Smith. He is usually the first to admit this fact to anyone. Today, Will takes time to understand how to treat a woman like a lady; he does whatever it takes to make his relationship work. He has even confessed to reading books on relationships to make him understand women better.

The relationship between Will and Jada is so open that Will can say to Jada that he thinks Beyonce is beautiful and he finds her attractive. She in turn can tell her husband she finds "The Roc" (Duane Johnson) attractive and they will laugh about it. Neither of them will then make it their mission in life to seek out those people they are attracted to in order to have an affair with them and dump their spouse, like a Brad Pitt would. This is clearly one out of several good reasons why they are still very happily married today.

Ironically Will and Jada are good friends with Tom and Katie, maybe that will turn out to be a good omen for the latter.

JOHN TRAVOLTA

Oprah's favorite man, John Travolta is also another example of a man that puts his family first. He is crazy about flying and has gone out of his way to involve his wife (Kelly Preston) and kids in a hobby so dear to his heart. He flies them all over the world at the drop of a hat, who does not want to be married to someone like that.

It was a pleasant surprise to see them together at the Stadium in Australia cheering on the Australian National team in a crucial soccer game just before the World Cup. If that is not a sign of togetherness and sharing, I don't know what is. His idea of a good time would include various surprises for Kelly such as breakfast (or in their case brunch, because John is apparently not a morning person) at home and dinner in another Continent or a day of pampering at the Spa for both of them.

In all their years of Marriage in a place like Hollywood, there has been no hint of a scandal of any kind. He is the ideal husband for most women who value stability and peacefulness in their lives without having to forgo having fun with their significant other.

BRAD PITT

It is quite clear that a man or woman that behaves like Brad in a Marriage can never make it work, plain and simple. Even if he marries smoking hot, smoldering, full lipped, luscious bodied, seven years younger than ex wife, Angelina, tomorrow, he will surely still stray sooner or later. If it is part of his make up as a human being, then we should expect him to dump Ange for the rave of the show business world in 2012 or thereabouts.

Magazine reports in far away Australia are already publishing that Ange has been telling close friends (apparently she does have some), that she suspects Brad of cheating because he is exhibiting signs of checking out emotionally from her by immersing himself in work and charitable endeavors.

Am I the only one that feels that for a man already in his forties, Brad has a lot of growing up to do still. Maybe, having kids may help to settle him down and make him finally realize that he is really not 'Tristan' in 'Legends of the Fall'. Remember, he has himself confessed to being somewhat of a drifter in the past, according to the London Mirror interview of his, recently published.

Another pointer or indicator which lends credence to the theory of Brad's fickleness is the number of times he dyes his hair to match those of new partners or girlfriends.

Anyone that knows anything at all about Mr.

Pitt will agree that he tends to 'visit the Salon' more frequently than the average woman does. He gives the impression of one who becomes too easily and too quickly bored.

Fortunately or unfortunately for him, he has picked someone that may make it difficult for him to make a smooth transition depending on who you talk to. Members of his family also seem to have major reservations as deciphered from utterances made after the break up, but they are trying not to say too much in public to show their anxiety so as not to upset him, in my view. This probably explains why Brad's Mom was so reluctant to cut off from Jen completely. The poor woman is probably wondering if her son has lost it completely.

Recently, his Grandma, Betty Russell who is eighty two years old was quoted as saying on the issue of Marriage to Angelina that " Brad promised his last wife on their wedding day that they'd be together forever and they didn't make it. He is a sensitive soul who just wants to make sure he can keep his promise this time around".

Her use of the word sensitive aside, something tells me Grandma knows her grand son very well indeed.

In life, a man can choose any of the options of

the men examined in this Chapter. It is up to Brad now; the ball is firmly in his court. If it is true that a man is shaped by his life experiences, then one might argue that Brad's relationships with women may still be affected by all that he encountered in his earlier days in Hollywood when he had to accompany strippers all over LA in limousines, in order to make ends meet. He may therefore not be in a position to recognize a gem in someone when he finds that person. Since he has already parted ways with Jen, we will just have to wait and see what happens with Ange in this relationship or in his future relationship(s) if any.

From all indications, it would have to be said that he is doing more than his fair share to make this particular relationship work (obviously the growing brood has a lot to do with this), although it is still early days yet.

14

The Beat Must Go On, It Always Does!

For Jennifer Aniston, the early part of 2005 must have been painful, tortuous even. It seemed there was nowhere to hide and grieve in peace and solitude. The World was having none of it. She was forced to come to the realization that her husband had left her for another woman despite all his denials and protestations. As it turned out, not just any woman, but the one that gets any man she wants.

She even admitted throwing little pity parties for herself frequently during this period. The speed with which her ex husband seemed to fly into Angelina Jolie's arms was not only hurtful it was also demeaning. Certainly not a self-esteem boost for any woman, no matter who you are or where you are from. The denials seemed more like a further attempt to mock and humiliate as much as possible. You somehow got the impression that each time Brad and Ange were photographed together in Africa, Europe and everywhere else, being very cozy and the denials swiftly followed from their reps that they giggled between themselves and had a lot of rib cracking moments as a result.

In the midst of all that, Jennifer started filming "The Break Up" with Vince Vaughn. The title of the movie was a mere coincidence but the timing was spot on. Jen and Vince apparently got on very well. Not too long, the rumors about a relationship between the two started. Jen, however needed time to heal and she refused to take the bait.

Was the filming of this movie at this time, the title and her co-star in the movie just what the doctor ordered or a God sent reprieve. Whatever it was, it certainly came at the right time for Jen and really helped her to find closure on arguably the most painful experience of her life.

Jen decided to give Vince a chance and she embarked on a relationship with him. On the face of it, people were saying stuff like how can Jen go from Brad to Vince? My own answer to that is also in the form of a question: How does Ange go from Billy Bob to Brad? The point being that Brad and Vince are as different as Billy Bob and Brad. I mean Ange was so smitten with Billy Bob and he is as different from Brad as Seal is to Prince. I know some people are thinking Ange upgraded whilst Jen degraded. Even Vince, tired of all the intrusion and the jabs recently stated that the media is desperately looking for a way to write him out of the script, implying that he also senses that they all feel that he is not deserving of Jen. I humbly beg to disagree with the school of thought that Vince is not good enough or man enough. Looks are not and should not be 99% of a relationship, as the Brad faithful seem to believe. Of what good are Brad's looks to Jen now, since he gave her heartache, despair and ridicule.

You look at a Vince Vaughn, a true man, a teddy bear, very comfortable in his own skin, not hair dye crazy, not obsessed with abs and it makes you realize that Jen was probably smart to have decided to have a relationship with him.

Ironically, actor and comedian Chevy Chase was quoted recently to have referred to Vince as 'looking like the refrigerator guy' in the ads for "the Break up". In reality, Brad was the one who was a refrigerator guy in his early days in Hollywood.

Another ironic twist is the fact that Vince was also in Mr. and Mrs. Smith and probably saw first hand how his new love's ex misbehaved not dreaming that he was going to be the beneficiary of Brad's excesses.

Not to get completely carried away however, because Vince did have a reputation for being a one night type of guy, no long term relationships of note that we know of. That suggests a commitment shy, George Clooney type, probably the last thing Jen wants or needs at this time. Confirming to Oprah not too long ago that he has not yet discussed the topic of kids with Jen at all also seems to indicate that they are probably taking things slower than the media expects, going by all the engagement reports that keep surfacing about the pair.

One thing Vince definitely had going for him is that he really made Jen laugh; Yes the old cliché is true. From all accounts, Jen even confided to her pals that she has laughed more since she met him than she did in the past ten years of her life (considering she was on Friends, that's saying a lot), sorry Brad. Would Vince know how to be in a long-term relationship? Does he even desire such a relationship, i.e. long term? Would old habits come between him and Jen? Will Jen ever really get over Brad and will she be able to trust another man completely? Once again we will just have to wait and see.

In the event that the relationship with Vince does not work out, of course am not wishing for this to happen at all, but it is Hollywood after all. I personally would like to see Jennifer with Prince Albert of Monaco (that is if he is still single of course). She has the qualities to be a worthy successor to the beloved Princess Grace in my opinion. Imagine Brad and Ange avoiding France forever because of Princess Jennifer! Wow.

Sadly, before we could finalise this publication, the majority were proved right yet again when "Vaughniston" announced their split. Hope neither party has any major regrets about getting together in the first place

Who knows how things could have turned out between them if Vince had won the role of 'Joey' on Friends which he auditioned for all those years ago. They may have never had a romantic relationship or they may have had one which may have led to marriage which might have prevented Brad and Jen getting together, Who knows? What is clear is that the journey of life does take different twists and turns indeed.

On a brighter note, this now frees Jen up for Prince Albert, seriously. If Jen is feeling a little to wary about venturing so far away from Hollywood for good, I would also want her to consider a certain gentleman by the name of Scot Foley. I have made this suggestion not because we all know he already has a certain fondness for that name but because he strikes me as one of few down there that can give Jen the stability and genuine love she so much deserves at this point in her life. I only hope he has finally gotten over Ms. Garner. He is surely a better bet for Jen than that trophy girlfriend, chest baring, 'suddenly bicycle crazy' Mathew that recently expressed an interest in her, but what do I know. I just wish she could have some joy in her love life, but you know what they say, no one person can have it all, there will always be something missing somewhere. I don't know if it's much consolation that she made the Forbes list as the tenth richest woman in Entertainment.

On another front, Congratulations are in order for Jen on her directorial debut in which she directed the likes of Robin Wright-Penn and some other Hollywood heavyweights in a very short movie titled 'Room 10' an experience that Jen herself has described as full of enjoyment for her. She apparently also recently paid a princely sum for a piece of prime property in Beverly Hills, which is under renovation.

She has clearly picked up the pieces and is forging ahead with her life, good for her. Yes, it's true what we hear so often, the beat always goes on.

15

A Look At Marriage And Showbusiness

The words Marriage and Show Business should never be used in the same sentence except of course for very few exceptions.

The rate of divorce is phenomenal, the average number of years for a show business Marriage is two, and that may be stretching it a little. What is the percentage of Hollywood couples that are still together, more like a fraction. Why you ask, do they bother? We need not bother contemplating the ones that last for mere hours.

Young Hollywood in particular, are guilty of trivializing something that should ordinarily be held as sacred and everlasting. You look at jokers like Pamela Anderson and Kid Rock and Britney Spears and Kevin Federline and you want nothing more than to ask them and others like them about the state of their mental health on the day of the ceremony (or in Pamela and Kid Rock's case, four ridiculous ceremonies), specifically.

Nowadays, the Reality TV couples are the latest ones making a mockery of the institution. The Jessica Simpson's and Nick Lachey's and the Carmen Electra's and Dave Navarro's who say their vows in front of television cameras and then commence work on several projects that will keep them apart most of the time. The only time they came together was in front of cameras for their shows.

As for Travis Barker and his soon to be ex-wife, words might be inadequate to sum up those two and their ill fated union.

Really, who is surprised when such unions collapse? It is most unfortunate that people just wake up and get married for the fun of it. You would think that it's the A listers getting carried away but no it extends to the D listers as well; it must be something in the water.

A typical example is Ms. Tori Spelling, daughter of the late legendary TV Producer Aaron Spelling. He controlled a fortune estimated at half a billion dollars. He was the Producer of such successful television shows like Charlie's Angels and Dynasty. She got married in a lavish ceremony that cost over One Million Pounds Sterling, (about One and a Half Million Dollars). The Marriage lasted barely fifteen months. She then decided that she preferred another woman's husband, Canadian actor Dale McDermott.

He of course promptly left his wife of about twelve years and their two children, for her. At the time her father was on his death bed, she was busy having her husband's ex wife ejected from an Awards show in Canada, the latter's own Country, on the flimsiest of excuses (something about a restraining order). Ms. Tori is apparently now selling all her old possessions (clothes, shoes, jewellery, sunglasses, etc) on ebay to raise some much-needed cash, how ironic is that? Now that new hubby has discovered how very little her inheritance is, we wait to see how long the Marriage will last.

Or take the case of the 'Newlyweds' on MTV,

who could have guessed that the Marriage would end so soon after the TV show and that Jessica would promptly be replaced by a member of the MTV family, Ms Vanessa something or the other who just happens to be best friends with the very shallow Debbie Matenopoulos of that famous E Network. The fallout of this is that Jessica is now suddenly sickeningly obsessed with her own boobs, to the extent that she now does everything possible to unleash them in public, at random. In my unsolicited opinion, if someone (a stylist) is being paid to dress her that way, they deserve to be relocated to a Zoo perhaps. Whatever happened to Jessica's religious upbringing. All rather pathetic.

Maybe there should be an age restriction on Marriage in Hollywood. There should also be a sobriety test to be carried out at the venue as well as psychological tests on some people who clearly need it to determine if they know what they are doing. Such measures should help weed out the Pamela Anderson and Kid Rock types and help bring back some respect and dignity long lost to the institution.

Even at the end of the union, most of these characters still don't get it. Instead of selecting the more accurate "incurable insanity" as the real reason for the divorce petition on the Form itself, they usually opt to hide behind the two most commonly used words in Hollywood "irreconcilable differences".

In all seriousness, is it not about time that the Officiating Ministers at such ceremonies start being held accountable for joining together two "certifiable loonies"? I mean clearly the Official that joined Britney to K-Fed or anyone ready to join together the disaster waiting to happen in the persons of Kate Moss and Pete Doherty should not be allowed to get away with such questionable conduct. There should be a means of keeping track of their Marriage Register to fish out marriages conducted for people unfit to marry. Such people must then be stripped of their powers (authority) to officiate at weddings, so that at the very least mankind is spared from the usual fallout.

Just Say No!

Would it not be great if such people want to marry and there is no one willing to help them do so?

Another jinx, albeit a surprising one for Hollywood unions is the Oscar prize. Winning Mr.

Oscar (that gold statue that is not easy to come by) now spells a death knell to previous seemingly blissful unions. The trend now seems to be once the female member of the union wins an Oscar, the Marriage disintegrates. This trend became noticeable after Kim Basinger's Oscar win. All of a sudden a nasty divorce ensued. This was followed by Hilary Swank and Chad Lowe's union. They were together well over a decade but the Marriage could not survive a second Oscar win. One must give credit where it is due right, at least it survived the award of one.

The latest one, surprise, surprise is the union of Reese Witherspoon and Ryan Philippe. Who saw that one coming? I certainly did not. She won an Oscar in March 2006, they are separated in October and have since filed for divorce, wow. What is it with winning an Oscar, we all know the odds, how extremely difficult it is for an actor to attain this prize in their Career. Why is it then that at the time they and their partners should be savoring success and reaping the rewards of hard work and all that, they decide to go their separate ways? And why is it that separation occurs more often when the woman wins the Oscar?

Could this have something to do with the age old male ego being too bruised to recover or does the woman suddenly become in my opinion, too J.Loish in outlook to everything, making life or the union suddenly a tad uncomfortable or unbearable for her hubby? We do not have any research study to rely on for answers but it is really one to ponder. The answer or answers are not that clear cut either. For this reason and this reason only, may you never win an Oscar dear Jennifer Garner, with love from a true fan.

You cannot help but wonder whether some of these guys have any idea at all how much they have been blessed. To have a wife who shuns the 'Paris Hilton' lifestyle, who brings so much into the union and who is not doing a 'Montgomery Shepard' with your best friend behind your back is really a BLESSING guys, not a curse. You need to be doing your utmost to hang on to such a person, man or woman.

The Jennifer Aniston's, Halle Berry's or Reese Witherspoon's strike me as just what Mummy would have ordered from God. Why then do the Brad Pitt's, the Eric Benet's and the Ryan Philippe's do their utmost to ensure the end of such unions? Why do these men suddenly choose to be so shallow? How bad can these women be really? How unbearable can life be with them? If one accepts that no one is perfect and that these men must surely have shortcomings of their own which their spouses were willing to bear, why are they (the men) being so short sighted? For most of these drifters it is always a case of learning the hard way.

Why then is the rate of divorces in Hollywood spiraling out of control? Its getting to the point where one is tempted to say to one's kids that they are going to be groomed to grow up and become a Divorce Attorney in Hollywood or a Plastic Surgeon also in Hollywood or play Professional Sports, (you just know they are gonna be set up for life because its beginning to appear as if any other careers outside these three are no longer worthwhile).

On a lighter note, I tend to agree with someone like comedian Mark Curry even if he was joking when he said that he would never have left a Halle Berry, no matter what she did. In his own words, "even if she wanted to do it with the neighbor, or he discovered her doing it, he would merely request that the guy leave his pyjamas alone and give them adequate time to finish doing the nasty". Obviously Halle has proven that she is not the type to misbehave that way but his point is well taken that it would have taken something massive from her for him to leave someone like that and even at that he might still be hanging around instead of leaving.

In spite of the remarkably poor record of Marriages in Hollywood, fortunately, there are some married ones that still bring a smile to our faces. They make us believe that there is still hope and all is not lost.

Joanne Woodward and Paul Newman: What can one say about the legend himself Paul Newman and his wife Joanne Woodward who have been married since 1958 (believe it or not that's FORTY EIGHT YEARS and counting). Well done guys for making the institution of Marriage all that it was meant to be and more. Apparently not all Las Vegas ceremonies are doomed.

Kelly Preston and John Travolta: They have been married well over a decade. They have two offspring together. In all those years they have both made the required efforts to remain committed to one another and to keep their family intact. They have both been able to manage their Marriage and Careers successfully. They are happy as a family. They both work regularly with people that are labeled as hot and still go back home to each other. Its called discipline. They show us that the ability to recognize what is important is still present in Hollywood.

Jada Pinkett-Smith and Will Smith: Does Will not make you want to be Jada? He certainly makes me sometimes wish I was. Emphasis on sometimes, because I do love my husband and I adore my kids. But the way he carries on with her and the way everything is with them is really Wow! Enough said.

Felicity Huffman and William H. Macy: There is something about this couple that just makes me smile. They are very comfortable with each other, they are extremely supportive of one another and you just sense that neither one is likely to do anything crazy that will jeopardize their Marriage. I recall that Bill Macy will be the first to happily tell you that the H. in his name stands for Huffman. How cool is that?

Kyra Sedgwick and Kevin Bacon: Longevity sometimes speaks louder than words ever will. These two are perfect examples. The same goes for Tom Hanks and Rita Wilson and Warren Beatty and Annette Bening and Sean Penn and Robin Wright-Penn and all the other couples (unfortunately not too many) that have stayed together for the long haul and through the good times and the bad.

Sarah Jessica Parker and Mathew Broderick: You can tell that this is a couple that understands perfectly what Marriage means and why they entered into the union. They have also been together for over a decade. They are one of the more quiet ones especially Mathew.

Tracy Pollan and Michael J. Fox: This couple have been together for a very long time. They have supported one another in health and in sickness, a rare quality in Hollywood.

Dana Reeve and Christopher Reeve: Mere words are inadequate to describe the union of these two. The love they shared was beautiful to behold. Methinks the word Dana may in fact soon be in the Chambers dictionary next to the words love or devotion. Sadly they both left us too soon.

There are also some recent unions worth mentioning such as:

Jennifer Garner and Ben Affleck: I expect a lot of oohs and ahhs with this one, but I tell you if they pack it up anytime soon, I might be the one visiting a shrink. The reason is that with certain people, you just know that they belong together and with these two that is what I sense. I saw them in 'Daredevil' and knew they would soon figure it out for themselves and they did not too long after. As for Ben, how many successful men do you know in 'Ego' land sorry Hollywoodland that would openly admit that they do not know what their significant other sees in them. He is a cool dude.

Nicole Kidman and Keith Urban: Nicole has proved that there is life after a terrible break up. One that came out of the blue just like Jennifer Aniston's. She handled the break up from Tom Cruise and the aftermath with plenty of poise and dignity. She even won an Oscar shortly thereafter. Everything culminated with her breathtakingly beautiful and wonderful wedding in Australia to fellow Aussie, and country crooner Keith Urban recently. She has moved away from Hollywood and all its trappings to Nashville to set up home with Keith. One cannot help but be very happy for her in particular and for them both, especially coming not too long after watching her ex husband of nearly a decade making himself the subject of Worldwide ridicule over a woman almost half his age.

Although Keith has recently checked himself into Rehab to battle his alcoholism, and this has been a source of ridicule in some quarters, the fact that he is making the effort should be commended and not discarded because a lot of people choose to live in denial. Instead of pretending, he is trying to make himself a better human being and ultimately a better husband for Nicole. Good on you, Keith.

Marcia Cross and Tom Mahoney: This does not appear to be a typical Hollywood Marriage. Both of them are in their forties and it's a first Marriage for both. The bride is an Hollywood insider, the hubby is a Stockbroker, very far removed from Hollywood. They are both very successful in their chosen Careers. They are both quite mature lending credence to the fact that they know exactly what they are doing and what they want out of life at this time of their lives. The latest news that they are now expecting twins is really icing on the cake for the couple.

Two For One: Congratulations are also in order for that yummy McDreamy, Patrick Dempsey and his wife who are expecting twin boys, wonderful news indeed. Correct me if I am wrong but methinks it would be very hard for a man to ever leave a woman that will soon be gifting him and the World two more McDreamys' to adore. GREAT STUFF.

Recipe For A Lasting Marriage

It seems that a very good recipe for having a long marriage (at least by Hollywood standards) would be to fly all your mega rich, superstar friends to another Continent and mingle them with some Royalty then proceed to have a week long lavish and stupendously expensive Wedding Gala. That way you are forced to stay together a good number of years because the mere thought of facing all those V.I.P's and the rest of the 'envious' World to tell them its all over after a year or two must be daunting even for Mr. Tom Cruise. For TomKat's sake though, I just hope J.Lo has not jinxed the whole thing by her presence.

A HOLLYWOOD RARITY

An extremely rare occurrence in Hollywood in particular and everywhere else in general is that of a wife who has been with a struggling actor for several years and has kids with him, then suddenly leaves on the verge of him becoming a very wealthy superstar. That was certainly the lot of highly talented, very good looking and always immaculately dressed black actor, Terence Howard whose wife left him reportedly for her High School sweetheart after several years of marriage and three kids, on the verge of him being nominated for an Oscar and becoming a household name. The reason this is so rare is because it is the absolute reverse of the normal trend anywhere.

The man usually (more often than not) dumps the woman that was with him during the struggling years for a 'Bimbo' as soon as the money starts rolling in. Ala Russian billionaire and fellow soccer fanatic Roman Abramovich who is reportedly currently very happy to part with billions of dollars to his soon to be ex wife who presumably stood by him when he was nobody and had five children for him, in order to be free to date one of tennis star Marat Safin's ex trophies, sorry I meant to say model ex girlfriend. I sincerely wish someone had told me back then that modeling really is the surest short cut to fame and fortune before I spent all those years toiling for two Law degrees. You have to give it up for the guy though, because to willingly part with BILLIONS of DOLLARS for any reason whatsoever not relating to a business deal of sorts definitely puts him in an extremely rare category of human being yet to be defined, or does it not?

Strangely enough, Terence ended up dating Marc

Anthony (Mr. J.lo's) ex- wife who had suffered a similar fate but the relationship did not last. It is worth mentioning however that Terence and his wife (ex wife) apparently seem to have always had a turbulent union resulting in an earlier divorce, a re-marriage and now a separation. In spite of all these, he claims he still wants her back. I am guessing that there must be something really special about that woman. Either that or Terence needs to be told that he is overdue for that appointment with a shrink asap.

16

Salute to Honor and Courage in Hollywood

W hen discussing a good Marriage or a great Marriage, you realize that it sometimes requires a lot of luck as well. I mean when choosing that person, the one you want to marry, the one you hope to spend the rest of your life with, you never know whether you will get lucky or not because it is once you are both in the union and things begin to happen and all that, that you realize whether you have been blessed or have made a huge mistake.

This is because Marriage is usually shaped by how the partners choose to handle situations that occur during the union. Most often the Brad Pitt option is employed, that is the option of bailing out at the first sign of trouble or if things are not going according to one's perception or expectations or simply because of an attraction to a third party. This explains why the divorce rate is so high, nowhere more so than in the Show Business World where it is sometimes difficult to separate art from life and where often times one imitates the other.

Marriage it seems is definitely one of the biggest gambles on Earth. A person puts their eggs in the same basket as another and you hope they keep their own end of the bargain as it relates to "egg giving and sharing". Oftentimes, Marriage fails because one party could not fulfil his or her own portion of the bargain to give or share. This is usually due to human nature or human weakness, take your pick. It always leads us back to the Garden of Eden and Adam and Eve and if only this and if only that.

Sometimes the way things will go is pretty clear right from the onset of the relationship however. For example, if your daughter introduces her boyfriend to you as 'T Pain' or '50 Cent', you know right away that she is either in for a very rough ride or some very cheap sex. In your mind, you must be hoping that she did not inherit her poor judgment from you. At the same time, if you pass the buck on genes, are you then admitting that her father's decision to marry you was inept.

Just like a 'secret', once more than one person knows about it, it is no longer a secret in the strictest sense of the word. Marriage requires more than one person in it and therein itself lies the problem. Two people will always bring different things to the table, no matter what, that's just the way the cookie crumbles. Even identical twins do not see every single thing the same way. Human beings are by nature very weak and it takes a lot to make a relationship between two separate and distinct individuals work. Most often as human beings we succumb to any number of weaknesses, some created by our own actions and others created by circumstances, albeit never beyond our control. As humans, we usually simply choose not to exercise that control.

Having said all that, it is heartwarming to note that special people still exist in our midst even though they are very few indeed, (extremely rare). It really seems hard to believe that such people actually occupy this planet, especially 'Planet Hollywood'.

There are however a few people (particularly women) that possess these wonderful qualities that one as an outsider believes cannot possibly exist in such a place.

It is quite refreshing and very encouraging to know that they in fact do exist in some. It is not possible to mention all those possessing these sterling qualities out there but for this write up I wish to mention two very special women from our list in the preceding Chapter, in addition to one other special one.

The first is the late beloved Dana Reeve, wife to 'Superman' Christopher Reeve who died from complications resulting from being wheelchair bound as a result of a horseback riding accident which occured in 1996. This is a woman that loved her husband unconditionally and displayed strength, integrity, courage and utmost loyalty in the wake of utmost adversity and bad fortune.

In circumstances where a lot of people would have found a way to desert, to disappear or to neglect, she chose to display love, compassion, support and dedication to a wheelchair bound husband. She did everything with a smile on her face. There is no doubt that her selflessness and dedication helped in no small measure to make her husbands last years on Earth worthwhile and joyful as much as was possible under extremely difficult circumstances. She also provided a source of hope to millions of wheelchair bound peopleWorldwide through her very vocal support for embryonic stem cell research and funding to help find cures for paralysis.

Very very sadly though, she died on the 6th of March 2006, having succumbed to lung cancer as a non-smoker.

She is truly one for the ages, a member of a very rare select breed of human being. I salute and admire Dana Reeve for the exemplary and truly remarkable qualities she displayed in her lifetime.

The second person I wish to mention is actress Tracy Pollan, wife of Michael J. Fox who has also been a very supportive spouse to her husband ever since he was diagnosed with Parkinson's disease. She has shown him that they are in it together for the long haul and has no doubt helped him to be in a position to face his illness with a stronger frame of mind and spirit.

The third person is Anne Lopez, wife of actor and comedian, George Lopez. Anne donated a kidney to her husband at a time when he was gravely ill and needed a donor. This was a very courageous and selfless act. Although some people seem to think she had no choice as he was the breadwinner, I on the other hand believe that was the more reason for her not to have done it as she was likely to be in control of a fortune if he was gone. By choosing to help save his life, she displayed enormous bravery and true love for her husband.

George Lopez definitely struck gold when he married Anne because I do not know of too many spouses existing anywhere that will gladly do what she did for him so willingly, myself included.

One cannot say enough good things about people or more specifically, women like Dana, Anne and Tracy. One can only hope that the younger generation will try to emulate people like them more, instead of embracing all that is the opposite of what they stood and still stand for as we so often see being reported on Networks like 'E'.

17

Some Questions We All Want to Ask the Parties

1. Hey Brad, on a lighter note, are you relieved "My Super Ex girlfriend" was not released before you dumped Jennifer?

2. Hey Brad, would you still have left Jen for Ange if she already had your kids before Mr. and Mrs. Smith or if she was pregnant during the filming of the movie?

3. Hey Brad, is it true that you developed a

crush on Ange after you saw her on the red carpet with Billy Bob making out as if her very existence depended on his saliva?

4. Hey Brad, what would upset you more, Ange leaving you for a younger man or a woman?

5. Hey Brad, would you leave Ange if she was unfaithful?

6. Hey Brad, in the event of a separation from Ange do you think you will have a huge battle over the kids especially Shiloh (regarding custody) having seen first hand how unforgiving she can be?

7. Hey Jen, is there any chance that you will take Brad back when Ange dumps him? Or would that depend on your relationship status at the time?

8. Hey Jen, when Brad told you he left College two credits short of graduation, did you pause at all, did any alarm bells go off, did you think hmm better watch out for irrational behavior?

9. Hey Jen, do you regret not starting a family with Brad before he went off to film Mr. and Mrs. Smith?

10. Hey Jen, do you wish you had insisted on Brad not doing Mr. and Mrs. Smith with Angelina Jolie, especially since he seemed so eager, even before filming started?

11. Hey Jen, what is the real reason why you and Brad did not have any kids together in seven years, was it medical, psychological or deliberate and if it was deliberate, were you both in agreement or was it at your own insistence?

12. Hey Ange, what would you do if you find naked pictures of Zahara (when she is an adult) in Brad's bedroom ala Woody Allen? This question is being asked because in spite of the fact that Brad has also legally adopted her, we all know you are both in the line of business that does not discriminate against anyone who decides to marry their ex partner or spouse's adopted children.

13. Hey Ange, how does it feel to be the one that men always dump their significant others for, I mean, has this coupled with all the accolades on your looks gone to your head at all or made you feel superior to mere mortals like a Jennifer Aniston or a Laura Dern, for example?

14. Hey Ange, which is the real Ange, the one with Billy Bob or this completely made over one with Brad Pitt?

15. Hey Ange, did you ever think that you could grow up looking so much like your Dad and turn out to be so pretty or have you neglected to tell us about some Dr 90210 works carried out to enhance specific features over the years?

16. Hey Ange, do you think the time must surely come when you will start paying for some of the agony you have inflicted on other women or were you encouraged by Julia Roberts karma being the gift of a set of healthy twins after wrecking someone else's Marriage?

17. Hey Ange, when you say that Brad is a good guy, would you agree that he is only good to you but quite mean to some other people?

18. Hey Ange, if you were to bump into Jen (we all know how unlikely this is) but in the event of a slip up by your reps, what would you say to her or would you just pretend that she does not exist like you did on the set of Mr. and Mrs. Smith?

19. Hey Ange, if Brad were to leave you for another woman would you take it out on the

kids by taking them as far away from him as possible to live?

20. Hey Brad and Ange, what would happen if you both happen to fall for the same woman and depending on your respective reactions would a threesome be in the cards or never?

21. Hey Ange, forget condescending, mean spirited, publicity stunt and all the other adjectives that come to mind to describe your recent indirect invite to meet with Jen (if she so chooses). In the event of a most unlikely meeting with Jen however, would any of the following occur:

    a) Would you spill secrets to her on how spiced up and 'wonderful' your sex life is with Brad nowadays;

    b) Would you bombard her with pictures of the "World's Most Beautiful Family" especially those of the little tots and ask her when she will be starting a family;

    c) Would you attempt to educate her on the intricacies of an international adoption procedure to help prepare her for it in the event that she decides to veer in that direction some day;

d) Would you try to educate her on how to steal a man who appears on the face of it to be in a happy marriage with his best friend or any man she desires, for that matter;

e) Would you make sure that Brad is far away from that meeting;

f) Would you show her how to inject her lips at home;

g) Would you hold her hands and repeatedly tell her how sorry you are for screwing up her life;

h) Would you attempt to make a move on her, after all she is quite attractive in her own right; or

i) None of the above.

22. Hey Ange, will you ever confess the truth that you coached Maddox very carefully to drop the 'D' word on gullible Brad?

23. Hey Ange, do you ever return to the real World from the land of make believe because you seem to have convinced yourself (100%) that you had absolutely nothing to do with the derailment of Brad's union with Jen. In

other words, are you always in fairytale land as a result of your primary occupation?

24. Hey Ange, Even you as daring as you are could not have expected a divorce to result from the utterance of that simple word 'Dad', right?

25. Hey Gwyneth, yes you Ms. Paltrow, why all the praise for Brad lately, are you having problems on the home front i.e. is everything okay with Chris? If the answer to this question is Yes i.e. all is well with you and Chris, I assure you that problems will soon surface, if you are not very careful.

18

Conclusion

The greatest lesson of all from the love triangle discussed in this book is that in life you just never ever know what can or may happen next.

A person can make plans and build a home and start a family or business with someone they love and expect to be in their lives forever and just when they expect everything to fall into place, it all goes horribly wrong.

A lot of people will agree with me on this if not on anything else, that it is one of the most painful experiences in life when you still love someone and you discover that they never loved you in return or have stopped loving you or they just can't love you back.

You look at a woman like Jennifer Aniston, the type of woman who is beautiful by all standards. Everything Mom prays for in a wife for her beloved son. A wife who even brings in as much income if not more to a Marriage and is not loud or unstable by any means. Does all that matter, NO! Because your husband or in this case Brad still dumps you with a bombshell or for a bombshell, you take your pick.

Jennifer herself seemed to have a premonition that some things don't last forever because she did give the best quote at the premiere of the 'Goodgirl' in 2002.

Best Quote - Jennifer Aniston

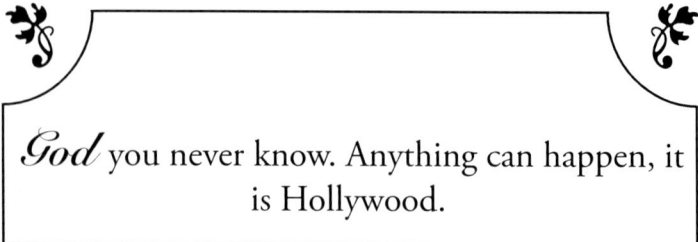

God you never know. Anything can happen, it is Hollywood.

This is particularly true in Hollywood, probably more than anywhere else in the Universe. The saying 'stranger than fiction' applies in Hollywood more than anywhere else. I mean, this is the sort of place where someone like the original 'Lois Lane' Margot Kidder, would have to run and escape from a homeless man on the streets, who was attempting to rape her whilst she was wandering around apparently suffering from loss of memory brought on by bi-polar disorder. I am not in any way trying to make light of this illness, but how strange is that story which actually happened in real life.

Oftentimes, the one who is the beneficiary of all the seemingly good stuff, the largesse as I like to refer to them, which could be anything at all, (that person who immediately seems to have the upper hand) needs to be a bit wary because in life it is always true that what goes around sometimes comes around.

After all is said and done however, the beat must go on, it always does. Life must continue and one should always strive to make the best of any and every circumstance in which they find themselves, we all owe it to ourselves to do just that.

If one were to ask Jen what the whole experience has taught her, knowing how humorous she is most of the time, I would not be surprised if she says something like these:

In a relationship, men and women do speak a different language often. Once in a very long

while, one is lucky to find one of the opposite sex that consistently speaks a similar or familiar language i.e. both on the same page. It seems that Brad and that woman seem to have a common language at this moment in time. Unfortunately for me (Jen), I was under the impression that Brad and I were both speaking American English, it turned out I was the only one speaking that language. Brad, apparently was speaking afrikaans all along and has now found a partner fluent in it. For most of us however, the search continues.

To end on a very light note, there is hope for all single mothers on the planet now, thanks to genius Angelina Jolie. Once you set your eyes or your mind on a man you fancy (married or single) just send your child over to him to call him Dad and a marriage might be on the cards for you shortly thereafter, WOW.

Disclaimer

The opinions expressed in this book are strictly those of the author. The quotes are direct quotes from the people discussed or their official representatives that were made in Newspapers and Magazine articles or on Television at various stages of their Careers. Comments of the author are her personal take on the events that transpired as it played out in the public arena.

The views expressed herein do not purport to portray anything other than what they are, opinions of the author.

ISBN 1425112412